100 Ideas for Secondary Teachers:

Interventions

Laura O'Leary

BLOOMSBURY EDUCATION

LONDON   OXFORD   NEW YORK   NEW DELHI   SYDNEY

BLOOMSBURY EDUCATION
Bloomsbury Publishing Plc
50 Bedford Square, London, WC1B 3DP, UK

BLOOMSBURY, BLOOMSBURY EDUCATION and the Diana logo are
trademarks of Bloomsbury Publishing Plc

First published in Great Britain, 2019 by Bloomsbury Publishing Plc

A catalogue record for this book is available from the British Library

ISBN: PB: 978-1-4729-6325-3; ePDF: 978-1-4729-6326-0;
ePub: 978-1-4729-6324-6

2 4 6 8 10 9 7 5 3 1

Typeset by Newgen KnowledgeWorks Pvt. Ltd., Chennai, India
Printed and bound in the UK by CPI Group (UK), Ltd., Croydon CR0 4YY

To find out more about our authors and books visit
www.bloomsbury.com and sign up for our newsletters

This book is dedicated to all those hardworking teachers going above and beyond to make a difference for their pupils.

Thanks to my family and friends for all of your ongoing support – but especially to my mum and dad for all that you do.

Contents

Introduction

100 Ideas for Secondary Teachers: Interventions is for any teacher who wants to make a difference to the exam outcomes of their students.

Closing the gap is on every school's agenda. As a teacher, you are pushed every year to improve the results of your learners but no one ever really tells you how to do it! Regrettably, there are no quick fixes or silver bullets and unlocking the potential of students can be challenging at the best of times. This book contains 100 ideas that will help you along this journey and support you in creating an action plan for impact.

Children only get one shot at an education; therefore, it is a teacher's moral imperative to ensure that the right things are going on in the classroom to secure progress. Skim and scan the ideas here but do not try to implement them all. The crucial starting point must be to identify what needs to be done to make the difference to your students instead of trying to do everything. Failing to invest time in determining what will make the difference could lead to a distortion in priorities and too wide a focus.

The book is organised around common themes to help you locate ideas that are relevant or applicable to your classes. Part 1 includes evidence-based ideas to help teachers in preparing intervention plans that work. Part 2 is all about getting student buy-in. It gives teachers 'go to' strategies for building effective working relationships, tackling disengagement and raising aspirations in the classroom. Part 3 provides practical solutions for overcoming issues such as disengagement, disorganisation and poor attendance. Parts 4 and 5 get down to the nuts and bolts of helping students with literacy and numeracy. Part 6 shares strategies for raising the attainment of disadvantaged students across all abilities, helping teachers in closing the gap between pupil premium students and their peers. Part 7 contains ways of scaffolding, guiding and supporting revision in order to help SEND students to perform at their best in exams. Part 8 includes ideas for interventions to push grade 7–9 or A–A* students, sharing easy ways to build stretch and challenge into lessons as well as how to make the most effective use of homework to support mastery learning and purposeful revision. Part 9 includes ideas for ensuring that after-school interventions and homework make a difference. With your average student sitting 25 exams in Year 11, knowledge and memory retention are critical. Part 10 explores ideas for interventions around revision and revisiting knowledge and skills. Part 11 provides ideas for interventions around exam skills, including exam technique and strategies for reducing anxiety. The final part of the book, Part 12, promotes ways that teachers can disseminate interventions that work with other colleagues and build on successes for following years.

If you are a 'Tweacher', use the book's main hashtag #100ideas to share how you use any of these ideas. Of course, feel free to Tweet me directly @laura_oleary.

How to use this book

100 Ideas for Secondary Teachers: Interventions contains a collection of practical ideas for you to use to plan and implement your own action plan for making a difference to the students you teach.

Each idea includes:

- a catchy title, easy to refer to and share with your colleagues
- a quote from a teacher or student describing their experiences of the idea that follows or a problem they may have had that using the idea solves
- a summary of the idea in bold, making it easy to flick through the book and identify an idea you want to use at a glance
- a step-by-step guide to implementing the idea.

Each idea also includes one or more of the following:

Teaching tip	Taking it further	Bonus idea ★
Some extra advice on how or how not to run the activity or put the strategy into practice.	Ideas and advice for how to extend the idea or develop it further.	There are 85 bonus ideas in this book that are extra exciting and extra original.

Online resources also accompany this book. When a resource is referenced in the book, follow the link www.bloomsbury.com/100-ideas-secondary-interventions to find extra resources, catalogued under the relevant idea number.

Share how you use these ideas in the classroom and find out what other teachers have done using #**100ideas**.

Preparing for intervention

Part 1

How to pick your battle

'How can I know what they need from me?'

All too often, as a teacher, your gut instincts determine the approach you take with students. Before planning your course of intervention, consider looking at evidence to help inform you about what will make the difference to your students.

For all your classes, you need to know the proportion of students making expected progress, the proportion exceeding expected progress and the proportion falling short. You should know which of your students are SEND, EAL (English as an additional language), PP (pupil premium) and below grade 4 and/or grade 5, together with the progress that these specific students are making. Do you know this? How do you know?

As if this wasn't enough, you should also know the gaps in achievement between these groups of students. Do you know whether the gaps between the different groups in your classes are closing? How do you know this? How are you ascertaining all of this information? Are you just referring to your gut instinct or to singular pieces of evidence, e.g. data?

Don't decide at random what is going to make the difference for your students. Instead, carry out your own mini-investigation using multiple pieces of evidence. Use the outcomes of this to inform your intervention planning.

Before deciding on your course of intervention you should audit your current practice to determine what's working and what's not. Here are some trigger questions to consider:

- Speak to parents. What do they think will make a difference? Do they know how they can support their child at home?

- Speak to your students. Do they know what they need to do to achieve their target? What do you think will make the difference? Why not hold your own pupil progress meetings?
- Look at other data about the student. Are they on track in their other subjects? If so, find out what other teachers are doing that is working – better still, see whether you can observe their lesson.
- Look at your mark book – what is the data showing you? Which areas of the specification are students struggling with?
- Look at any past papers that students have completed – what types of question are they are losing marks on?
- Look inside your students' books. What do you see? Are notes complete? What do your plenaries and assessments show?
- Speak to other staff. Is it a teaching issue? Is it a pastoral issue that is causing a barrier? Or is it exam anxiety?

Look at the learning environment. What will make the difference? Typically, quality assurance is something that is done to teachers. For instance, you may have been observed as part of a learning walk by your line manager or had to submit books for a work scrutiny. The purpose of gathering this information is to understand your classroom. You don't have to write a report on your findings or complete any pro forma. You do, however, have to ring-fence some time to reflect on the questions above and decipher what you could do that would make the difference to your learners. Otherwise, it could all be pointless.

You need to take a diagnostic approach to your intervention. For instance, it's no good planning extra revision sessions for an underperforming student if the learner is disengaged in your actual lessons in the first place. This idea is about making the time to come up with a clear plan and identify what actions you need to take to have an impact on student outcomes, rather than railroading on and trying to do it all.

> **Bonus idea** ★
>
> Carry out this process with another teacher. Pair yourself up with a critical friend, someone who will tell you whether what you are intending to do will actually make a difference. Consider sharing your findings and ideas with other teachers.

There's no 'I' in team

'It is good to have everyone singing from the same song sheet.'

There is no substitute for teamwork when it comes to getting the best out of students. Effective action planning requires the right people in school to work together.

Everyone in school wants the same thing: the absolute best for students. Therefore, if everyone in your school wants the same thing, there must be a collegiate approach to achieve this. If everyone is working solo, there is the real risk of teacher or student burnout – especially with students who could face being pulled from pillar to post. Pastoral and curriculum staff need to work together to consider the barriers to student learning. If a student in your lesson isn't making progress, why? It is vital that you determine this reason for the students you teach. You could deliver all-singing, all-dancing lessons from 9 am till 3 pm, but if attendance is the underlying issue for a student, investing time in improving your teaching won't make a difference. Similarly, if you are teaching a disaffected or passive learner, it is no good pushing them into extra intervention classes. They'll turn up but they may as well have their eyeballs painted on.

Look at each of your students and consider the barriers to their learning. Look to share your information with key stakeholders such as form tutors and key pastoral staff. Propose that a system be created for effective information-sharing between all staff and suggest setting up a focus group to tackle issues affecting Year 11 in particular. There are no quick fixes; closing the gap requires a planned course of action rather than everyone trying to do everything.

Taking it further

Create a way of sharing key information regularly. This might be through a dedicated slot during staff briefing. Consider a whole-school action plan to improve Year 11 exam outcomes and suggest CPD with the sole focus of sharing best practice around Year 11 intervention with the SLT. For instance, staff could share any 'lightbulb moments' – strategies that worked with past Year 11s.

Bonus idea ★

Put forward the idea of key student speed dating: simply print out the photos of students who are not making expected progress, arm every member of teaching staff with a pen and give them time to write down any ideas they have that might just make a difference to each of the individual students. They could also share any information they have about the students' barriers to learning.

Make a plan

'Plans make me feel more in control.'

As a teacher, there isn't much more stressful than the run-up to final exams – often you end up feeling more anxious than your students! The only solace is in knowing that you couldn't have done any more in supporting and preparing them for their exams. A well-thought-out plan (perhaps set up as a countdown or calendar) of key actions is the most important piece of the puzzle in ensuring the best outcomes for students.

The beginning of a new half-term can be a perfect catalyst for putting new plans into action, and the earlier you make a plan the more likely success will be. Start with your whole school calendar. Know the exam date for your subject. Count how many lessons you have left with your students. Think about how many homework slots you have remaining and how many opportunities you have for revisiting content. Then think about your students. What will make a difference to them? Sit down with your departmental team to draw up this calendar – the greatest plans are formed in collaboration – not to mention the merits of sharing the workload.

On your calendar, have a dedicated space for recording the #100ideas strategies you will implement, and then identify a series of checkpoints. Practical checkpoints include:

1 exam dates (these are available from your exam board)
2 key dates for Year 11, e.g. study leave, mock and real exam dates
3 mapped progress towards completing the exam specification (where you should be and by when)
4 revision and what revision tools students should have ready by when.

Lighten the load

'If you always do what you've always done, you'll always get what you've always got.' (Henry Ford)

If you want your results to improve, there is very little point repeating things you have always done – unless, of course, that is because you know that they work.

Before trialling any of the #100ideas, your first thought must be: 'What can I stop doing that will give me the time to try something new and which could make a greater impact?' Here's a guilt-free list of things you could change:

- Guillotining worksheets: It may look tidy but it has zero impact on learning.
- Marking: Don't mark every page; get students to tick and flick each other's books – it's great SPGST practice (spelling, punctuation, grammar, specialist terms).
- Homework: Every so often, set a reading, thinking or watching task.
- Tidying up: Schools have cleaners. Could they help by sorting books or book shelves?
- Use your prefects better: If you don't have any, create the role. Slip them your photocopying code or, better still, get them their own!
- Consider curriculum planning: Draw up a workload planner and make sure your priorities are where/when they should be.
- Cap any Key Stage 3 assessments to one page: At GCSE, candidates in most subjects are given one page to formulate the majority of their extended answers. Get Key Stage 3 students to plan, draft and peer-mark, but the work they submit for teacher marking should be no more than one page. And when students do hand in their book, get them to open it on the page that needs marking.
- Use strategies such as live marking to reduce marking (see Idea 48).

Data matters

'Having this information at my fingertips helped me to focus my interventions.'

Being able to read and use data to drive improvement is crucial in determining what course of action to take with students.

Ever heard of Sherlock Holmes' mind palace? As a teacher, you have one – it's where you store information on your students' progress. There are, of course, lots of other useful places you store information about your students, e.g. the school data management system, in your planner, and targets in students' books. Pull them all together and ensure that you know the answers to the following questions about your classes:

- What are the target grades for your students?
- What are your predicted outcomes for your students? How does this compare to student target grades? In order to achieve those grades what grade boundaries are you using?
- What are the overall trends for your key groups – is there a specific issue with your class? Think about different groups: boys v girls, pupil premium, SEND, EAL, one target grade below.
- As your data stands, which students could you have the most impact with?

It is worth tracking your exam classes and ensuring that you know the extent to which you are closing the gaps in attainment over time. Look at just that data for your Year 11 groups and decide on a focus group of no more than five students. You may have to make some difficult decisions and 'leave behind' some of those students who have learning traits that are out of your control, e.g. persistent absence. The next step is ensuring that data is actually used!

Teaching tip

If you have a school data manager, ask whether they have any spare time to put this information together for you.

Taking it further

The data you enter is only as accurate at the teacher who is entering it. Make sure you have clear moderation processes in place across your team to ensure that a grade 9 really is a grade 9. Consider buddying up with another school to compare accuracy in grade predictions.

Bonus idea ★

As teachers need to understand data, so do all stakeholders – do parents need a data guide?

Constant reminder

'Keeping on point every lesson is always a challenge.'

One way in which you can keep track of intervention needs is by utilising a desk planner.

If you are fortunate enough to command your very own classroom, sticky-tape your planner to your desk (a sample desk planner is available in the online resources). Your school may give you a list of key students who need to be targeted, or you can come up with your own ideas as to which students you believe you could make a difference to. Once you have jotted down their names, spend time thinking about their barriers to learning (make this specific to your classroom environment). The most critical feature of your desk planner is the space to record ideas for strategies for improvement. These strategies need to be doable within the lesson and it might be the tiniest of details that makes the difference.

Ten ways to make the most out of your desk planner:

1 Give your key students the best seats in your classroom – this tends to be at the front, close to the board.
2 After you have set a task, go to your key students first and check in. Have they understood the task?
3 Use your desk planner to monitor your questioning – EVERY lesson, ask all key students a question during feedback to check their understanding.
4 Live-mark or tick the work of your key students during the lesson.
5 During the lesson, make sure you explain to your key students how work could be adapted to make it revision-ready. Use

your desk planner and tick off the students who know how to revise and how to revisit content, and help the students who don't have these skills... yet.

6   Make a note on your desk planner of any student who is absent. Have notes ready to give them.

7   Have your desk planner in front of you when you are marking these students' books first and use your desk planner to record recent assessment data and test scores. Use it to make any comments on an individual's progress or teaching misconceptions for the whole class. Do you need to reteach?

8   Have your desk planner in front of you when you are planning or adapting a lesson.

9   Take your desk planner to departmental meetings and staff meetings such as CPD sessions – share, revisit and refresh your ideas! Make immediate notes of any practical ideas to improve your teaching and do them in your very next lesson.

10   Scan through your desk planner before your students arrive to your lesson.

> **Bonus idea**   ★
>
> Imagine the power of planning strategies for improvement with someone else or, better still, pooling ideas with a bigger group of staff. Get some good biscuits and invite like-minded colleagues to attend your desk-planner party. It will soon snowball.

Lesson planning for exam success

'There's so much content, I can barely find time for exam practice.'

When planning lessons, consider what a Year 11 exam candidate needs to be able to do in order to be successful in your subject, and then focus your planning around this single question. Try creating your next lesson with the following elements to ensure your learners are exam-ready.

Teaching tip

Create your own doodle pad, e.g. questions to put at the forefront of your lesson planning.

Taking it further

By deliberately exposing students to an exam focus every lesson, it ensures that they become familiar with the exam they will be sitting. Also, building in revision and revisiting tasks can ensure that students are revision-ready for when they finish the course.

Bonus idea ★

Sit down with a copy of your subject's exam papers and base your lesson planning on key features or things that students must be able to do to be successful in your exam.

Start your lesson with an **entry starter** – on the board or out on desks ready for when students arrive, to avoid any loss to learning. This is a great opportunity to revisit past learning – for example, through regular low-stakes testing. Set your **learning goal** in 'exam-speak' (Idea 33); this provides the opportunity for students to engage with exam language and unpick the meaning of command words every lesson. Remind students of the **big picture** – emphasise the importance of the lesson and why they need to learn this. Model how this might look like in the **exam** – show an exam question or a model answer. When delivering new content, **reconnect** and glean what students already know so that you can quickly diagnose what they don't know. **Introduce** new learning, ensuring the use of clear instructions. Give students the opportunity to **demonstrate** their understanding of new learning – have they understood it? Hinge questions are great for this. **Review learning** – can they apply their learning to an exam context? Finally, get their new learning **revision-ready** – give them a strategy to **memorise** their learning and/or create something to help with revision. Set a **home learning** task that provides opportunities for independent practice.

Getting student buy-in

Part 2

Phone home

'I was delighted to know his hard work is paying off.'

Sometimes a simple phone call home is all it takes to get students on board.

This strategy can be used as a carrot or a stick. A call home is such an overlooked method of praise yet probably one that has the most benefits. It is the quickest, cheapest and most personable way to get student buy-in.

Parents are important and keeping parents in the loop and engaging them with their child's learning can have a positive impact on progress. Most parents care about how their offspring are doing at school. Parents, on the whole, want the very best for their children. They can be a great tool for reinforcing your comments of praise or support. Whenever you get a moment (after school, lunchtime, free period), just give one child's parent a quick call to let them know how their child is progressing. Make sure you credit the effort their child is putting into the subject. Above all, point the parent in the direction of any exercise books or past paper their child has completed where there would be further written feedback for the child to read, which could then be reinforced at home. Use the conversation as a chance to praise the effort or work you wish the student to replicate. Aim to phone one parent a week.

It will take a few moments of your time but, particularly for those students who are sat on the fence of trying (or choosing not to try), it can really push them over onto your side. It is worth remembering that students tend to put the most effort into the subjects that they either genuinely love and are interested in or are taught by their favourite teacher, as they will typically want to please them.

Underpinning it all

'If you don't know your students, how can you possibly know what will help them to achieve their true potential?'

It is important to invest time in building effective working relationships in the classroom.

Research has shown links between student motivation and positive teacher–student relationships. It boils down to the idea that if a student thinks their teacher genuinely cares about them and if they are met with a positive and warm manner in the classroom, then they are more likely to engage with the activities happening in the classroom, which will positively affect their exam outcomes.

Similarly, how motivated a student is in your lesson could be determined by how the student perceives your expectations of them. For instance, if a student believes that you have high expectations for their achievement in your subject, then they are likely to be more motivated to meet your expectations.

The same rings true of students with low academic self-esteem and low confidence in their abilities at school. This may be linked to role models or the lack of importance placed on education and qualifications at home, so teacher–student relationships have a much greater role to play in raising the aspirations of disaffected students.

Why not be a secret advocate for your key students? Make it your business to know about any successes they have had outside of your lesson and drop this information into any conversations you have with them. Ask other teachers about the progress they are making. This can work wonders for improving classroom relationships.

Teaching tip

Always take the opportunity to greet your students at the door. Take the steps to discover what students want to do after they finish school so that you keep them focused on the bigger picture and where they are going, regardless of where they have come from. Most importantly, make the effort to speak to every child, every lesson.

Bonus idea ★

Get disaffected students to keep a learning log that records how individual lessons make them feel. Students should jot down every time they enjoyed a lesson or felt like they had learnt something. This can provide great evidence for what works for engaging tricky students.

Check in

'Once my dad knew to look out for the stickers, there was no stopping him.'

Parents need up-to-date information on how their child is progressing to be able to support them usefully at home. A couple of parents' evenings and a few report cards home are not enough. Engineer it so that parents have to cast an eye over their child's work regularly. This way parents know how their child is doing, along with exactly what they can be doing to help support them at home.

The Sutton Trust-EEF Teaching and Learning Toolkit highlights that the more that parents are engaged in the education of their children, the more likely their children are to succeed in the education system. School improvement and school effectiveness research consistently shows that parental engagement is one of the key factors in securing higher student achievement. Good questions to ask yourself include: 'Are you providing parents with clear and timely information on how well their child is progressing?' and 'Do you give parents guidance about how to support their child to improve?'.

Evidence from Ofsted suggests that a critical dimension of effective teaching and learning is the relationship between the teacher, their students and their parents. Don't forget that once a student has embarked on study leave (if this is an option), the main people involved in their revision will be parents.

Facilitating opportunities for parents to delve into exercise books is an effective way of ensuring that parents receive clear, specific and targeted information about what their child needs to be doing to improve in your subject on a regular basis. One method of achieving this is to have a way of ensuring parents are checking feedback students are given on pieces of work. This can be accomplished by using a 'check-in sticker' to make sure students are showing work and feedback comments to their parents. On to a sticky label, print 'Your child has been provided with **feedback** on what they need to do in order to make further progress. To encourage learning conversations in and out of the classroom, please review your child's work and indicate that you have discussed your son or daughter's performance by initialling this sticker.' This action builds a continuous home–school link and can help secure parental engagement. Good things to typically 'check-in with parents' include any tests students complete, practice questions or any self-review sheets. You could even provide students with sticky tabs and ask them to place one whenever they feel they have shown improvement or acted on teacher or peer feedback or targets for learning, so this can be flagged up to parents too.

For this strategy to have the desired impact on learning, parents must be given the tools they need to support their child. You must be mindful of this with any written feedback that you provide. Would a parent understand this? Would a parent be able to support their child with this? This is where access to online support materials or hard copies of revision guides can be divisive, especially if parents are unskilled in how to use them. Similarly, you need to think about how parents might support students with homework. If a student doesn't understand or is struggling with a homework task, have you put their parents in the best position to be able to help them at home?

Higgins, S., Katsipataki, M., Kokotsaki, D., Coleman, R., Major, L.E., & Coe, R. (2014). *The Sutton Trust-Education Endowment Foundation Teaching and Learning Toolkit*. London: Education Endowment Foundation.

> **Bonus idea**
>
> Always pass your school email address to parents or guardians to provide an instant home–school link. Better still, get their email address!

Write home

'Knowing the game plan made me feel even more invested.'

Who cares about your students more than you? Parents. Parents and guardians want the best for their children. Involving them in your plans can guarantee that students are doing what they need to do at home, so send a letter to give parents the heads-up.

One way to improve student outcomes is to involve parents. Parental engagement is key for ensuring that students are meeting their commitments outside of your lesson and it can prove to be a vital step for getting buy-in from students.

Things to include in your letter home are: exam dates, what content students should revise for each exam, details of what you are doing to secure their success, and, most importantly, things the student should be doing to ensure they reach their true potential. The letter might also include a revision checklist, instructions on where and how students can access revision materials, and guidance on revision – how much and how often, and how parents can help their children to revise Don't forget to include your contact details so parents can get in touch with any questions.

A letter home shows parents you have a plan for their children and it can also make for a very powerful conversational tool at parents' evening. Sending a letter home is a chance to make everyone clear on their responsibility and it can make life a lot easier. Team this with strategies such as 'check in', whereby parents continue to be signposted to written feedback and targets for improvement, and the job's a good one.

Taking it further

Parental engagement has been identified as one of the strategies that is key for closing the gap. Consider running parent workshops to develop positive revision habits at home.

Bonus idea ★

You could distribute your letters at their last Year 11 parents' evening, as this is typically well in advance of their child's leaving date. It's also usually the last chance to give students the kick up the backside they might need to make the grade.

Reflect on reports

'I used to hate parents' evening but now I find it really useful.'

Typically, parents get a report sent home twice a year. Annually, parents probably get one chance to sit down with teachers face-to-face. What happens after these events? What is the follow-up to them? What actions does a student have to take?

At the start of parents' evening, give every student a form to complete. The form should have space to record:

- subject
- teacher
- progress (on track or not)
- targets for improvement.

At the end of the parents' evening, every student would leave with a personalised action plan of what they had to do to improve. You could even add on a column for what parents or guardians can do to help at home.

This is a way of capturing exactly what a student needs to do in order to secure the best possible outcomes from their exams. Collect the forms in at the end of a parents' evening so that they can be photocopied and a copy given to every stakeholder: parent, teachers, form tutors and student.

Encourage parents to stick their summary from parents' evening on the fridge to help prompt a conversation about progress at home. Encourage them to delve into their child's exercise books for further feedback.

Similarly, when it comes to reports, pastoral leaders should encourage students to reflect on any report data they receive. Why not, after every report, make it a form-time activity for each student to make an action plan as to what they are going to do to ensure progress?

Teaching tip

Make sure that all the parents you need to see have appointments. If a parent genuinely can't make it, curtail your appointments early and then use the time to phone home instead so you have communicated the necessary information to the right people.

Bonus idea ★

Plan for your parents' evening like you would a lesson. Consciously think about handing out revision materials to parents so that they leave with everything their child needs to revise at home. Make sure each departmental area has a display stand showing what good revision looks like. Signpost parents in the direction of any revision books or tools that would be helpful to their child.

Find out from them

'Sometimes the best informants are the customers.'

When thinking about what could make the greatest difference to a student's overall grade, one of the best places to start is asking students for their suggestions.

Teaching tip

If class dynamics mean that you don't want to ask such questions to every student, carry out the activity in a student voice group and capture a snapshot.

All too often the phrase 'students should be working harder than the teacher' is bandied around. While in the classroom this is true (learning should be hard), the reality is that both teachers and students should be working hard! After skimming this book for golden nuggets, make your first stop your students. Pose to them the following question: *'As your teacher, what else can I be doing to help you to achieve your target grade?'* Equip each student with a sticky note and ask them for at least one realistic suggestion. Give them the chance to discuss this in small groups to be able to choose the best ideas to try.

Taking it further

It is just as powerful to ask students: 'What things do I do as your teacher that are making no difference to your progress?' Obviously as their teacher you will know best, and some suggestions (such as giving up practice questions) are just not going to float. But sometimes you may learn that you have been investing your time in something that is pointless.

This activity might provide you with affirmation that you are doing a grand job, especially if students are unable to think of anything else you could possibly be doing. Or it might just throw up a gem of an idea that could make a real difference. When I asked a group of my Year 11 students this same question, they came up with some surprising suggestions such as that they actually wanted to do more exam questions but under much stricter time conditions, like in their final exam. Implementing this idea did not require any more planning on my part but has proven to be a great addition to lessons.

Keep it positive

'It helped me to know that my teacher believed in me.'

After you have marked a piece of work, spend 30 seconds writing down what was awesome about it. Expressing to students what they are good at can encourage them to build on these talents, which can then help to reinforce their strengths.

Everyone likes to feel good and know that they are good at something. For instance, a student using lots of specialist terms would be commended by the teacher. The student will then link your comments to success and the likelihood is this student would then go on to repeat their behaviours. If you teamed this with a target that could further enhance the student's use of specialist terms, then they will be motivated to act on your feedback.

Next time you are marking a set of mock papers, think about how much time you spend jotting down things that will improve student answers. Then look at how much time you spend writing down the things they have done well. If students' achievements are overlooked, you can run the risk of them not doing those things again. Strengthening things that students are already good at can actually lead to very easy wins when it comes to extra marks. It is easier for a student to improve on something they are already good at than to work on something that they find hard. Aim to compliment every student in your class regularly. If you are time-poor, create marking codes for this!

Teaching tip

Next time you are marking a mock paper (which takes ages anyway), spend 30 seconds writing a sticky note for each student on what they did really well. Stick it somewhere for the student to find. For instance, you could put a sticky note for every student under their chair so they have to get up to retrieve comments on everything they did well. Then challenge students with the question: 'What can you do to build up your existing strengths even further?'

Bonus idea ★

Next time students are doing a peer assessment task, give them one minute to write down positive comments only. Play a cheesy feel-good song while they do this – 'I Got You (I Feel Good)' by James Brown should do the trick!

Map it out

'The map is a reminder of where they need to go.'

This could be a way of showing to your students where they should be on their learning journey and by when.

Shown at the beginning or end of a lesson, a map can really help to keep students focused. It is also a handy way of showing students how much work or exam content they still have to get through, emphasising the importance of making every lesson count as well as highlighting the significance of attendance and ensuring they don't miss anything.

It doesn't take long to make the map and it is something that is reusable; you might even be able to just use your school calendar. It could be worthwhile giving students a copy so they can shade off what they have done (a sample lesson map is available in the online resources).

This can be a great tool for manipulating and motivating students into working harder every lesson or doing homework tasks, as students will be able to see exactly what has to be done and by when. It is an effective alternative to an end-of-term party.

That winning feeling

'It was great to be able to raise students up rather than knock them down.'

Imagine a day in the life of a grade 3 student. There is the very real possibility that they spend all day being told by different teachers that they are failing. If that was me, I wouldn't care much for school. The message here is simple: treat every lesson as a clean slate and as soon as possible praise any student who is showing traits of being a disaffected learner.

For some students, failing can even become the thing that they are good at. You then run the risk of a student playing the class clown and not even bothering to try, as being the class clown and being happy to fail is preferable to trying and then still failing but not getting the laugh.

Similarly, some teachers will treat students based on preconceptions formulated from experiences of previous lessons or influenced by reputations of students or views from other teachers. Where possible, create opportunities for students to be successful in your classroom. This can start from the moment they enter your room. Always greet your students with a smile, ask how they are and be quick to praise them wherever you can, even if it is for the smallest of gains. Focus on a glass being half full wherever you can. Aim to treat all students with unconditional positive regard and treat every lesson as a clean slate. This can be really powerful for disaffected students as praise is often showered on the most able or best-behaved students. Consider setting tasks that weaker students will be able to complete successfully, and then commend them on their achievements before moving them on to something more challenging.

Teaching tip

If a student is doing great, let parents, form tutors and heads of year know. The more people that can be tagged into good news, the better.

Bonus idea

During a lesson, jot down positive comments linked to how well students are learning on a sticky note. Focus your comments on the habits you wish them to do more of and discreetly drop it onto a student's desk or stick it onto the back of their chair or school jumper and then get a peer to read it out to them. You can always get other students to write the comments for each other, too!

Capture success

'This was easy to set up, grows organically and looks amazing!'

Whenever you spy a student working hard, putting in an impressive amount of effort or demonstrating a skill desirable to learning, snap a photo of them at it. Print off their photograph and then stick it up on the wall.

Teaching tip

For some students, it might be their worst nightmare for their photo to appear up around school. For teenagers who are of the shyer variety, why not set up a mini-wall in your classroom where reviewers of the photographs are just their friendly peers? Or send more wary students a secret note. Put their photo in an envelope with the reason why their learning stood out and leave it in their book for them to discover.

Taking it further

Set up rewards for 'revision heroes'. Anyone caught revising or making excellent revision materials should be celebrated.

Getting adolescents to buy in and commit to trying their absolute best every lesson can be one of the trickiest jobs for even the greatest of teachers. The typical school award system usually motivates only the youngest students.

This strategy works best when you have a popular area around school that you can use to display photos. Free up a wall space along a busy corridor to put up your photos of hard workers in action. The more staff taking part in this activity the better, and the greater your display will be. Ideally, get hold of a school camera that can be used solely for this purpose. On labels, scribble down the reason a student's photo has made it up on the wall – you can pick up speech bubble stickers cheaply online. When jotting down comments, tap into the idea of positive psychology and praise students on the learning behaviour or skill you wish to see them replicate again in the future.

It can be a really nice touch to keep parents in the loop too and give them a heads-up that their child is being recognised for their hard work. Pre-made stickers are also great for this. Create yourself a generic template sticker for this purpose that can be quickly stuck into a student's planner or in their exercise book. As well as taking action shots, snap away at pieces of work and showcase them on the wall too, annotating each piece with comments about what makes the work worthy of the wall!

Aim to update your photos frequently. Or even better, save yourself the time and give this job to prefects to do. Changing the display often will ensure it is meaningful for students and guarantee that they are keeping a lookout for their own face or (more likely) the faces of their mates. A useful tip is to give the wall a catchy title such as 'Excellence in action'. An added bonus is that this is a quick and easy way to spruce up scruffy-looking corridors and can really capture the interest of any visitors to your school.

Checkpoint questionnaire

'The questionnaire helped me to start some difficult conversations.'

Students are complex creatures. As well as facing the challenge of sitting life-changing exams, students have to also deal with adolescence: a tricky period of life. It is worthwhile checking-in with one-to-one conversations or reflection worksheets. Sometimes a combination of the two can work best.

Share any concerns immediately with the pastoral team!

It's not always easy to pick out reasons why a student has plateaued. This idea can be a great way of finding out any issues affecting students straight from the horse's mouth, so to speak. Unpicking whether student issues are pastoral or academic can be helpful for tailoring intervention plans.

Why not create a 'checkpoint questionnaire'? It provides an opening for students to reflect on the progress they are making and it can open up conversations about barriers to learning. Student wellbeing is everyone's job, and one of the things that needs to be avoided at all costs is student burnout. In some schools, students are pulled from pillar to post, committed to extra lessons and lunchtime, break-time or even breakfast interventions. Mental happiness and ensuring that students don't suffer from 'school stress' are essential and, as a teacher, you have a role to play in keeping check on how your students are feeling about their learning in your subject.

Factors you may wish students to reflect on include:

- student understanding of subject content
- detail of class notes
- content and organisational skills.

A final open-ended question will give students the space to put across their own ideas about things that are affecting their learning. Students will not necessary spill their guts onto this questionnaire but it does provide an opening to have a caring conversation, giving you the chance just to touch base and ensure that every student in your class is dealing with the pressure of your subject.

Removing common barriers to achievement

Part 3

Student wellbeing

'The first step is noticing there's a problem.'

In a society where the number of students with mental health issues is growing, it is important that you consider students' wellbeing in all you do.

There are a growing number of students who deliberately self-harm, or struggle with eating disorders, self-esteem issues, anxiety, depression or stress. You have a role to play in supporting students to be resilient and mentally healthy.

- If you spot unusual behaviour you must pass this information onto the appropriate person within your school so that the relevant member of staff can take suitable action.
- Within the classroom, promote ways in which students can manage stress, such as through exercise.
- Where relevant, especially when students are revising for things such as mock exams, remind them of tactics they can use to manage stress – for instance, having regular breaks during revision or chatting through any concerns they have with a teacher.
- Be deliberate in planning for pre- and post-exam care. Avoid giving students time to compare results, grades or details of how much revision they have done with their friends as this can lead to more worry!
- Promote the importance of eating right and getting a good night's sleep to fuel body and brain! Encourage students to exercise and take regular breaks from revision.
- When doing mock exams or practice questions, share ways to deal with any feelings of panic or anxiety. If students find themselves beginning to panic, encourage them to sit back in their chair for a moment and focus on their breathing.

Organising the disorganised

'I didn't think I'd ever see the summit of Mount Paper.'

For some students, a barrier to revision, let alone the exam, can be their organisation of the overwhelming amount of paperwork that is generated in each subject.

As a teacher you will know which of your students struggle with organisation. These are the likely candidates who, before they can even get on with their revision, will have to tackle Mount Paper. And just like Everest, only the most committed will survive; the rest will just give up.

The severity of a student's disorganisation will determine your potential course of action. If a student is failing to look after their book, treat them to a bit of sticky-back plastic to keep the outside of their book in tip-top shape.

If a student arrives to your lesson bookless then a heavy-handed approach is perhaps required. Why does a student keep forgetting what they need for your lesson? If it is forgetfulness, a punitive measure may help them to remember it.

But what if a student's context is different? What if a student's home life is so difficult that it is a miracle they even make it into school? Take the burden of organisation away from these students and give them a place to store what they need for your lesson in your room. Make sure it is somewhere accessible so that they can just grab what they need when they arrive at your lesson. Where possible, give them homework on separate sheets. Offer time after school or over a lunchtime for them to complete their homework.

Teaching tip

It's amazing what a nicely presented book on the outside can do for the work on the inside. Especially with a little positive reinforcement: 'Christopher, your book is looking great. Make sure you underline your date and title to keep it looking organised. It will be great to revise from.' Similarly, in the last few minutes of every lesson ask your students, 'Could you revise from your notes? Can your peer revise from your notes?' Then give them a few minutes of time targeted at sharpening up their books so they are revision-ready.

Taking it further

When marking, start with looking at the books of your most vulnerable students and make sure these books are organised. Have glue at hand and stick in any loose sheets. If you have a TA in your lesson, don't forget to arm them with a glue stick!

What's the point?

'I don't care!'

Sometimes you end up with a student who, for whatever reason, does not give two hoots about your subject, let alone passing the exam. No matter how much you try to coerce them, sometimes a student cannot see the opportunity they are throwing away. This can be especially frustrating if the student has the talent or ability to do well in the subject. The only thing you can do in this situation is to remind them exactly what the point is.

Legacy

Try giving students two sticky notes. On one, students write down what they will be doing one year from now. Do not accept 'Don't know' as an answer. Remind them that they will be doing something. On the other, students imagine it's one year from now and write down how they want to be remembered by you as their teacher. These questions are powerful as they force self-reflection on what the student wants for him or herself. It makes them consider their legacy. No one wants to be remembered badly. As a last resort, it can be worthwhile looking at how a fresh start can be orchestrated. As a surprise, keep the sticky notes and give them back to students before they leave school.

Action boards

Action boards are a spin on the idea of a dream board – a collage of images or words that someone hopes to see or have in their future. This is a great activity to suggest to the pastoral team at your school. Every student could create a collage of all the things they hope for in their future life as an adult. Once students have put together their action board, get them to create a border to provide space for writing down the key actions they must take to make steps in achieving the contents of their board. Central to these will be qualifications.

Tracking absence

'It would be great if they didn't miss lessons in the first place!'

Keeping on top of absenteeism is important. It is useful to come up with your own way of keeping a record of those students who have missed a lesson and what exactly they have missed. A slight adjustment in the way in which you use your teaching planner can really help you with this.

The average full-time secondary school teacher teaches 11 classes. If each class is full, the typical teacher will be delivering lessons to over 300 students a week, although this may vary according to the curriculum time allocated to the subject that you teach. How is it possible to keep track of students who are absent from lessons? There are ideas in this book that can support you in achieving this but how do you administrate it? It can be a paper-shuffling nightmare, and provide students with an excuse to escape extra work.

Attendance of lessons is now usually recorded with electronic software. While it is possible to sift through systems to find out which of your students have missed which lesson, this task can be very time-consuming. One way to track student absence is to keep a list of who missed what lesson. But in my experience, lists prove to be much more of a hindrance, especially when lost under mountains of marking.

An alternative approach is to use your planner to record such notes. If a student is absent from your lesson, flip to the date of that class's next lesson. Make a note of the student who is absent. Having this jotted down on the date for the following lesson will act as a reminder to yourself to follow this absence. If you make a note on the day of the lesson the student actually missed, you may miss it!

Teaching tip

Missing a lesson could prove detrimental to a student's final outcome. Murphy's Law dictates that the learning students miss will probably be of necessity to the exam, so use this technique with your Year 11 classes first.

Bonus idea ★

Why not put a folder up on your classroom wall marked 'Catch-up work' and use it to put in the names of any absent students, along with the work or notes that they have missed?

Getting them into school

'School's boring, why would I bother?'

You can plan as many all-singing and all-dancing lessons as you want, but if a student is bunking off, they can't learn anything! Use these ideas to draw attention to persistent absence and flag up your concerns.

There are many strategies that have already been mentioned in this book that will go towards improving attendance – for instance, creating a caring culture in your classroom and investing time in your teaching and learning. If attendance is an issue, try suggesting these ideas to the people in school responsible for attendance:

- Keep parents in the loop about the importance of attendance at every possible opportunity.
- Publish a child's attendance figures on any report data sent home. Use a red, amber or green system to indicate student attendance measures. For example, attendance of 89% might not seem so bad to parents but if it was shaded in red this would flag up that their child's attendance is poor. Make sure reports are put in the hands of parents via the post rather than relying on students to hand them over. Reissue parents with a copy of their child's report on arrival to parents' evening just in case they didn't receive the initial copy – this also makes for much more meaningful questions from parents.
- Consider calculating predicted grades based on a child's attendance figures.
- Equate attendance percentage to the number of days their child has actually missed from school and likely impact on their results.

- Include information about the impact of non-attendance on attainment as a header or footer on any letters or reports sent home. Get this information put on the homepage of your school website. Have it up on a whiteboard screen in the main hall during any parents' events.
- Make sure teachers have up-to-date statistics on student attendance for any parents' evenings so that they also push for improved attendance.
- Set up a home–school agreement that is specific for Key Stage 4. Highlight the importance and impact of attendance, along with procedures for catching up on any work missed through absence.
- Ask students what would help to improve attendance.
- Show students the difference improved attendance would make to their predicted grades. Demonstrate this by using examples of past students.
- Attendance rewards systems can be effective. Ask your students what would be a good reward for 100% attendance or for best improved attendance and don't rule out hard cash prizes.
- For persistent absence, look at putting in place a positive reintegration plan, such as a return-to-school meeting to welcome them back and offer any support they may need.
- Set up a compulsory homework club for poor attendees to repay hours missed.
- If your school has a mini bus, could it be used in the morning to collect any students that find it hard to get into school? It would only take a few mornings of the scariest member of SLT fetching students to motivate them into making their own way to school!
- Issue transport passes if students need them.
- Get form tutors to hold attendance meetings with students in their tutor group. Every child in school should have a target for their attendance.

Taking it further

At parents' evenings, members of SLT should book 'attendance meetings' with parents of children whose attendance is poor to add weight to the importance of students being in school.

Bonus idea

Think about providing poor attendees with permission to skip some homework if they attend school – having them in school is better than them staying at home.

Absence makes the heart grow fonder

'It was easier just to go to school and avoid the hassle to be honest.'

What should happen if a student misses one of your lessons? Do you follow up their absence, and provide them with the work, homework, questioning or exam practices they might have missed? If you answered 'no', then you are missing a trick.

Your school will have an attendance policy, but what should you do if and when a student misses a lesson? Your first priority must be shifting the focus and accountability of catching up onto the student. **What actions must the student take if they miss their lesson?** Generally, it is a real pain if a student is absent from a lesson, especially if the lesson is part of a sequence. You must be consistent with your approach to absenteeism. After reading through the following steps, you may find it helpful to turn them into a poster and put your expectations up on the wall of your classroom for all to see.

- Have catch-up work pre-planned, linked to a revision guide or textbook.
- Invest some time in creating a revision workbook for the complete qualification you are teaching. This will take a large chunk of time but will pay for itself in the long run.
- Make the revision guide accessible online for students to download and print themselves.
- Make each section of the revision workbook explicit in terms of what content it is covering.
- Each section of the revision workbook should contain the theory, knowledge or skill required for the exam, followed by activities for learning. Organising revision guides like this will make for easy catch-up work by simply pointing students in the direction of the part of the revision workbook they have missed.

Get them in and on!

'There just aren't enough hours in the day!'

You can easily risk losing the first few moments of your lesson to a staggered entry. Instead, make it the expectation that on arriving to your lesson, students are to sit down immediately and complete a task.

The most efficient entry tasks should encourage students to either revisit past learning or make connections to whatever they will be learning about in that given lesson.

Position yourself so you have one foot in your classroom and one out in the corridor. Give each student a friendly welcome to set the tone for learning, along with instructions to complete the task on the board. Putting yourself in this place guarantees that students are not delayed in getting their bums onto their seats and doubles up as a handy opportunity to police uniform. You should only have to do this for a few lessons before students get into the routine of getting in and getting on.

Be strict with your timing. As soon as the first student has finished the entry starter, move on. Having an activity that students have to complete immediately helps them settle and stops them dawdling.

If a student misses an entry starter due to lateness, ask them to complete it at lunch or as homework. Students will soon get into the habit of arriving to your lesson on time and ready to learn!

Be sure to jot down in your planner the names of students who are always punctual and quick to get on with the routine for learning. Reward them. A phone call home or something edible goes down well.

Teaching tip

Always include an additional challenge task just in case students' arrival is really staggered. Why not try adding challenge and super-challenge tasks?

Taking it further

It can be great to build this routine into other things that might chip away at lesson time, such as collecting in homework. Add instructions to get homework out onto the board. This will ensure every student has it out ready on their desk.

Bonus idea ★

Enforce the expectation that if a child arrives late to lesson they must sneak in and sit down like a ninja so as not to disrupt learning.

Priorities

'This is a manageable way for students to get ahead of the revision game.'

What if your subject is bottom of the Progress 8 bucket list? What if your subject is not a student's priority for revision? By taking time in lessons to shrink and summarise learning, this idea provides a stress-free way to get students revision-ready.

Teaching tip

This activity works really well when students are encouraged to compare their summaries with other students. Why not build in time for students to trade sticky notes or magpie ideas from each other?

In most cases, instead of using high-level and detailed notes created in class, many kids will opt for the easier option of an off-the-shelf revision guide when it comes to exam season. Arguably, although revision guides can be useful, they are not as detailed as the notes that students may have completed in lessons. So, here lies the trick... make it the harder option for students to use generic revision guides.

- Plan ahead and break down student learning into chunks. Once students have reached the end of one chunk of learning, build in time for them to complete the activity of shrinking their work down onto one side of a sticky note.
- Students should skim and scan their notes, highlighting key ideas, specialist terms and key facts.
- Challenge students to shrink their learning onto a sticky note. Underpin the task with clear success criteria for what should be included on it. Or better still, model a good example!
- After completing their sticky note, students should stick it into their books directly on top of the notes that they have condensed. Ta-dah! A ready-made revision card!
- For any disaffected student who is not opting in, explain the time that they will be saving themselves in the long haul. Their Year 11 self will thank them for it comes to exam time.

Bonus idea ★

Why not test their prep? As an activity, give students an exam paper or exam question and get them to self-assess whether their condensed summaries would enable them to answer the questions.

Mix it up

'Putting the weakest students with the strongest teachers makes the difference in my class.'

Some students would make more progress if they were taught by a different teacher or were in a different classroom dynamic. If this is the case and there is the chance to have a bit of a mix up of classes, do it.

Almost all teachers will do all they can for their students, but sometimes you can find yourself teaching a class that you struggle to gel with. Or it might be that you teach a class with a few students who have put a wall up against your charms. If you've done all you can when it comes to securing student progress and it still isn't working, or if you are at the point where disaffected students are disturbing the learning of others, then it may be time to sit down with your department and discuss a more radical way forward.

A fresh start can be very powerful. A new teacher. Sparkly new exercise book. Different class peers. Changed learning space. A clean slate can be a great catalyst for engaging a disaffected student or securing greater progress for students who may have plateaued.

The best time to make such a transfer is at the very start of Year 11. A new teacher at the start of a new academic year fits in with the pattern students have become accustomed to throughout Key Stage 3. It is what they are familiar with.

Ultimately, the decision to opt for class changes will be decided by heads of departments and will depend on the flexibility of the timetable. Nevertheless, it is an idea that should be considered.

Teaching tip

Performance-related pay makes this suggestion a bit controversial. For instance, if a teacher had a perfect class made up of students who were all making fantastic progress, they would be fairly reluctant to give them up. But this is about the bigger picture, and occasionally that means changing the teacher face in front of them.

Bonus idea

Before the start of Year 9 or 10 (whenever your GCSE starts) when classes are decided, it is common sense to take into consideration the progress students have made with different teachers throughout Years 7, 8 and 9. It may even be worth asking some students to reflect on their teacher preference. (Do not do this explicitly. Instead, ask a general question about which teacher they felt they made the most progress with.)

The nuts and bolts – helping students with literacy

Part 4

Reading

'Speedy reading saved precious minutes, which I could use to check my answers.'

Regardless of subject, every exam paper requires students to read the question and, in many cases, this can be alongside further stimuli and/or sources linked to particular questions. In some cases, this can be pages of text. Every school should by now have caught onto the importance of promoting literacy and a love of reading.

Taking it further

Add the reading ages of your students onto your seating plans and ensure that you support students who need help with reading. The same goes for exam concessions – if a child in your class is going to have a reader in the exam, act this part wherever possible so that the child gets used to listening to someone saying the words for them. Take it one step further and find out from your SENCO who the child's reader might be for exams and see whether they are available to support during reading tasks. You could request their support for mock exams, too.

Schools are increasingly promoting reading through programmes such as Accelerated Reader, whereby students are given a choice of books to read from and, on completion of the book, sit down to answer questions on the text to check for comprehension and understanding. Similarly, whole-school initiatives such as DEAR (Drop Everything And Read) are being used by schools up and down the country to encourage children to read. However, how deliberate are you being in creating opportunities for students to read a set amount of text in an allotted period of time? Or how deliberate are you in creating the opportunities for students to read text similar to the sources they may be presented with in the exam? The reality is that children who can read quickly gain time on their peers. Similarly, those children with well-practised routines for dealing with large chunks of text are at the advantage. But it must be practised.

You must give careful consideration to what you want students to do as soon as they sit down in the exam hall and the invigilator announces that they may start their papers. What routine do you want your students to have honed ready for Year 11? For example, do you want students to spend the first five minutes of the exam reading through the paper? If so, you need to instil this in them through guided practice – skill and drill. A small start is to emulate this routine in your classroom. What do you do when you hand out a worksheet or something for students to read? Can you tweak your routine slightly to build in reading time – even if it is the deliberate practice for as little as one minute?

For longer pieces of exam text that children might need to read – do you practise this? If so, how often? During mock exams is not enough. Students need to practise things with the support of their teacher so that they know exactly what to do with similar pieces of text when they are revising independently at home or when they are faced with large chunks of text in the exam.

For a typical exam, work out roughly how much time students will have to spend reading text and make this part of your typical classroom practice. Create a routine for reading alongside any other exam habits you wish to promote in your students. It may be a worthwhile exercise to look at your exam and think about what you want students to be doing as soon as they sit down. What about when they first open the paper? With any insert booklets? When interpreting exam questions? After they have answered each question? After they have finished the exam? If they have any time left over? Be deliberate with these actions and practise them at every opportunity so that they become second nature. Start off explaining them to students – explaining *why* they are important so students buy in. Aim for these actions to become habits but be aware that some children will need gentle reminders and further modelling or scaffolding until it becomes part of their own typical practice.

> **Bonus idea** ★
>
> If you are getting students to read anything, always make it your default practice to ask students questions to demonstrate their understanding, or set an activity such as a subject-specific test to check comprehension.

PEE in the same way

'Taking a shared approach means students have greater consistency and more opportunities to practise.'

Most exam subjects require extended written responses to some questions. Spending a bit of time with your colleagues exploring a possible shared approach to this could really ease the burden on students and strengthen exam technique.

Teaching tip

Practise yourself. Use the same exam conditions and rules that students have to comply with to complete a practice exam question.

All subjects require candidates to generate written responses to some exam questions. PEEK, PEAK, PEEL, SEXC, 123 or just a straight up PEE are a few of the ways in which students are being taught how to respond to questions. So not only are they being expected to revise textbooks full of knowledge, we then expect students to go and sit an exam remembering to write in a particular format according to the subject. The average student sits ten GCSE qualifications and they may well have been taught ten different ways of structuring an answer. CRAZY!

Before deciding *how* students should answer an extended writing question, find out how your English department are going about it. Or look to the strongest department or faculty in your school whose exam requires written application. Carry out a mini-investigation. What rules are they teaching to students for written responses? Can they be transferred to your subject? Would they be applicable to your exam? Could just a slight tweak be made to the rules to make them workable in your subject rather than making up a whole new set? If so, piggyback onto an existing idea. A student who is taught only a handful of ways to answer an extended question will have the advantage of having more practice (as it will be built into a larger number of subjects), rather than being expected to learn a new method for every subject.

This idea could work well paired with a target bookmark. Students could be encouraged to jot down any literacy targets they could work on in any subject. Practice makes perfect!

If you find a common approach fits across several subjects, it is worthwhile creating a common slide or logo graphic that can be used in lessons to ensure that everyone is singing from the same song sheet. Applying a common logo could also support weaker students in making the connection between the transferable skills.

Once you have determined the rules for writing you are going to stick to, start to drill the skill. For instance, you need to first teach ways to ensure that students are consciously applying the rules for writing, and if they have enough practice at this they will then become subconsciously competent. If you are teaching students how to write using the rules of PEEL, always get students to write this acronym down at the top of the page or question, and once they have answered a question get them to highlight where they have done each of these things.

To assist in your delivery of the rules for answering a question, get students to follow specific instructions. Ideally get them to assemble something following instructions accurately, then share the same for answering an exam question.

The importance of literacy

'Easy marks can be lost in exams if literacy isn't prioritised.'

Every teacher is a teacher of literacy. Knowing that literacy matters should inform your lesson planning and you should aim to build in discrete opportunities for looking at pieces of work for SPaG errors and, in addition, ensure there are chances for students to learn and apply specialist terms to answers.

There are various ways you can build literacy practices into lessons. Here are a few:

- create a glossary for a topic
- peer- or self-assess answers for SPaG errors using mark schemes
- specialist terms spelling tests
- word-scapes (create pictures using just words)
- flash cards for keywords
- keyword Jenga™
- marking model or un-model answers (get students to decide which keywords they would add in)
- play dominoes or pairs to match keywords with definitions
- keyword charades
- spot the mistake in answers
- create word mats or connective pyramids to help students with sentence structure
- give students a list of key terms to be used in an answer
- active reading tasks
- literacy logs – students should jot down any SPaG errors they have made
- when completing practice questions, build in a minute or more for students to reread their answers to spot missed opportunities for using specialist terms.

Live literacy

'This really helped me to avoid common errors.'

SPGST: spelling, punctuation, grammar and specialist terms. This accounts for five per cent of the marks that go towards most GCSE qualifications. Literacy matters. If there is a word that is spelt incorrectly by more than 25 per cent of your class, you need to address this mistake.

Most qualifications require candidates to write extended answers, for which they are graded on their spelling accuracy and use of punctuation and grammar. This means you must opt in to marking work for literacy as well as subject-specific knowledge or skills. You must pick up on spelling mistakes and ensure students use dictionaries to correct mistakes.

Turn any SPGST errors into a poster. Include examples of the ways in which students have misspelt words in their work. Then give it some press. Address the mistake in class. Give students opportunities to practise spelling it correctly. Give your class a spelling test. Name and shame anyone who makes the same mistake in future! Keep them guessing as to who has made the mistake. If you put this up on the wall and refer to it in your lessons, you will soon have all your students checking to see if they were one of the offenders.

If you can get a group of teachers on board, every time one of you spots a serial mistake, knock up a poster and put it up in as many classrooms as possible. If you have space to spare anywhere in your classroom, you can build up the mistakes into a literacy wall. You could get your students to make the posters. You could even use pens that write on glass and jot down the correct spellings on the windows.

Teaching tip

After you have put one of these posters up, if a student repeats the same spelling mistake (and if the student is of the right disposition), take their photo with their mistake in a mug-shot style and put that up on the wall. Wherever you can, slip words that are commonly misspelt into example answers. Point these out, highlight them or spell them incorrectly yourself and hope a student in your class picks up on it. Nothing is more memorable to a student than when a teacher fails!

Bonus idea ★

When walking around the classroom during a lesson, highlight or circle any spelling mistakes you spy in student work and get them to make the corrections – if you have a TA, get them to do the same.

Sussing out specialist terms

'SPGST marks can nudge some students into the next grade.'

Students who are confident with the application of key terminology are most likely to bag themselves the most marks when it comes to use of SPGST (spelling, punctuation, grammar and specialist terms).

At the start of any course or topic, review the specialist terms you need students to be able to use confidently. Be systematic in your teaching and modelling of these words. Be selective with the terminology you want students to be using – always start with the trickiest words first, even if this means just getting students familiar with the words. The more you refer to the use of key terms, the more likely your students are to use these words.

S = Spelling

- When possible, whizz around the room checking student spelling of keywords – especially words you know students regularly get wrong. Make corrections there and then.
- Write the correct spelling up on the board and get students to check their own work.
- If certain questions in the exam secure extra marks for spelling, get children to build this into their answering routine. Be deliberate in getting students to do an action that means they are definitely checking their spelling and not just saying they are – for example, get them to change pen to check for spellings.
- Show students the importance of spellings. For example, for many exam boards it is five per cent of the marks – how does this affect grades? Does it equate to a whole grade or half a grade if these marks are secured? Use examples of previous students where this has made a difference to grade outcomes.

- Get students to keep a spelling log in the back of their book for any spelling mistakes – get students to regularly return to this and update it with spellings they have learnt. Then get a peer to test them on the words at a later date, or get peers to check their spellings against the spelling log for key pieces of work.

P = Punctuation and G = Grammar

- If students are making regular errors, these need following up. Make sure you explain the mistake students are making and give them the correction. It can be helpful to write down grammar or punctuation rules on a sticky note so that they can have this information out in front of them on the desk for future reference.
- If students are making the same mistake – for example, the incorrect use of apostrophes – then they won't just be making this mistake in your lesson. Do share this information across their teachers and with any TAs so that everyone can pick up and correct the student – it is surprising how quickly regular errors can be corrected if everyone is singing from the same page.

ST = Specialist Terms

- If a question demands the use of specialist terms, always build this into your routine for modelling how to answer any question.
- Regularly ask students, 'What specialist terms should be included in this question?' Then get students to list any specialist terms required in certain questions in the margin near which they will be writing – they can tick these off as they use them.
- After students have answered an exam question, get them to add up how many key terms they have used in their answer – challenge them to go through and increase that number by three or more.
- Regularly give students the task of revisiting key terms using an 'empty your brain' approach – be it as a starter or at the start of the routine for answering an exam question.

Bonus idea ★

As a school, you could make standard-issue correction stickers for staff to use when providing feedback on literacy mistakes.

Command words

'Students who understand command words are less likely to misinterpret the question.'

Students sit on average between nine and 11 GCSEs – around 30 exam papers. They will be exposed to the same command words in many of those exam papers. I don't know about you but if I was being taught the meaning of 'explain' by my English teacher, and then my geography teacher gave me a slightly different interpretation, I would get confused. Avoid this mistake by being deliberate in the teaching of command words.

As a body of staff, look at all of the definitions provided for command words by the exam boards you use and then pick the 12 most regularly used exam words. Agree on the definition of those commands words and agree to teach them using the same explanation. By taking this approach, you will ensure consistency in practice and improve student understanding of words such as 'explain', 'describe', 'define', 'discuss', etc.

Once you have agreed on the definitions of command words, build these into every lesson. Learning objectives, outcomes, goals, WALT, big questions – however you choose to set the scene for your lesson, aim to phrase it in the same way an examiner would. By setting the aim for every lesson using exam speak, you'll provide a chance to unpick what command words actually mean on a regular basis, guaranteeing that students become confident with the array of command words exam boards are now choosing to use. There are many ways you can use the lesson aim to provide the chance for students to unpick the command word:

- Through questioning, get students to unpick what they have to do, including identifying the meaning of any command words.

- Get students to write a title for the lesson in their own words based on what they need to learn.
- Give them a slip of paper or sticker with the lesson goal printed on it. Get them to annotate it with what the command word means plus any other restricting words contained in the lesson aims.
- Get students to write down the objective of the lesson, highlighting command word(s) and any restricting words.
- Make students generate a bullet-point checklist of everything they need to be able to do by the end of their lesson based on its goal – a bit like putting together a recipe.
- Flip the idea. Provide students with a lesson objective or aim that is missing a command word. Get students to decide how this might appear as an exam question.
- Try setting the lesson goal as an exam question, e.g. 'By the end of the lesson you will be able to answer X.'

Bonus idea ★
Have you ever given students a command word quiz, e.g. 'Define the command word "explain".' This could be a great way to avoid students misinterpreting the question. Similarly, with exam practice, what do you do as a teacher if a student has explained instead of described? How are you making sure that student never makes the same mistake again? Modelling work where students have made this mistake can work wonders!

Flip flash keywords

'A glossary of key terms just wasn't working for my students.'

Instruct students to write each keyword on a sticky note and stick them across a double page in their books. Students can write out the definition of each keyword underneath. Ta-dah! An instant revision tool.

Teaching tip

An alternative approach could be to get students to turn their keywords into exam bunting. Each student could be responsible for one key term and, once put together, these could create a masterpiece.

Use this activity as a flipped learning task or consolidation activity to revisit learning. Ask students to discover the definitions for each of the keywords you've given them for homework. Challenge students to derive their own list of keywords relating to the content and key ideas to be learnt. Be clear in your success criteria: each definition should provide a worthy answer of what could typically be a two-mark question in their exam. Then find opportunities for use!

- Before looking at the cards, make a list of all the keywords linked to a particular topic.
- Use the words written on the top of their sticky notes as a memory jogger, then try to remember the meaning of the key terms.
- Spend some time looking at definitions before covering up keywords, then writing them out. Look – Cover – Write!
- Play pairs using their cards – peel off the sticky notes and match them up with their meaning.
- Answer an exam question with the cards.
- Annotate a question with keywords that should be included within an answer.
- Use a highlighter to mark their work or a peer's every time they use one of the keywords.
- Play bingo with the key terms – pick a number of words to tick off as and when they are used during the lesson.
- Apply the principle of dual coding and get students to turn the keywords into a picture.

Bonus idea ★

Flip flash cards make for a great lesson starter. Give students the task of revisiting their keywords and then set up a tally chart to show who is able to use any of the key terms in their verbal responses.

Keywords league tables

'Competition keeps my students interested.'

Ruth Marsh (@SherburnGeog) is an advocate of using games to promote literacy. For example, using league tables can create a healthy competition in lessons, which can help engage all students but especially boys.

The purpose of this technique is to promote literacy and raise the importance of key terms. This is great for any ability group and gives immediate feedback, which boys respond to. It has many uses:

- as a starter to introduce new key terms (after homework to learn the terms)
- as a plenary to check understanding
- as an exam review
- as a revision tool at the end of a whole topic.

Create a spreadsheet with a column for student names, and next to this a column for each set of key terms you are testing. The technique works best if you test the same number of words each time – say ten. You can also add a formula to the spreadsheet so that it will update and recalculate the students in the lead automatically, or you can do this manually (a sample keyword tracker is available in the online resources).

Decide whether this can be a self- or peer-assessed activity and whether you want to include DIRT (Dedicated Improvement Reflection Time). Students get immediate feedback and can use this feedback to identify areas of progress or to develop.

This idea works most effectively when used consistently and when linked to students' personal targets, such as the use of key terms in their written work. This technique can be used as evidence that students are making progress.

Teaching tip

Try setting up a league table across different teaching groups to promote friendly competition. Give each class a name, e.g. Marsh's Masters.

Taking it further

This idea can be used as an effective tool to focus on closing the gender gap. This technique engages boys and allows them opportunities to succeed; this has been shown to improve their motivation in the lesson.

Bonus idea ★

Use of praise and rewards can be targeted and focused. The winning students can be rewarded, but so can students who make progress. It can be worked into your whole-school rewards system.

Break it down into steps for EAL students

'Chunking learning down into steps makes it manageable for EAL students.'

Most EAL students are capable of exceptional progress. However, unlocking a student's potential can be tricky if language is a barrier.

First, double check any exam concessions a student may be entitled to – if students are entitled to a scribe, reader or extra time, ensure that this provision is available for practice.

Consider the student's overall academic profile – which subjects are they are on track to pass? Speak to their teachers in other subjects to discover approaches that might be working elsewhere. If the student is below target and struggling across all subjects, speak to their pastoral leader, as students should not be set up to fail – support should be put in place. Also check that EAL students are sat in the right place to support their learning – not at the back!

- Make sure EAL learners have a dictionary available for translation should they need it.
- Sit them next to a student with a high target grade in English so they can become more familiar with the language.
- Place a whiteboard next to the student so that you can write down a reminder of key instructions for them. Better still, prepare instruction reminders in advance.
- If you have a TA in class, ensure they are checking in with the student.
- Encourage discussion and talk in English at all times between peers.
- Consider the use of knowledge organisers for revision – focusing on the bare necessities in the first instance.

The nuts and bolts – helping students with numeracy

Part 5

For tricky numeracy questions...

'These strategies helped my students avoid panicking.'

One of the key things a teacher must do is to prepare students for what to do when they quite literally don't know what to do. Giving your learners the strategies to cope with answering tricky questions is a vital skill – and this can particularly be the case with tricky numeracy questions that may have children in a panic.

Teaching tip

Why not create an acronym with your class or a set of instructions to follow if they get stuck with any question? Creating it together will make it more memorable for students. Model its use at every opportunity to make it a habit. For example, get students to write the acronym at the top of any exam question and be deliberate in following the steps. You could even select an acronym that could work across any subject.

Bonus idea ★

Check your specification and audit past papers – what percentage of the marks comes from calculations? If a student is really struggling, make sure you are strict on setting them a time limit for answering a numeracy question.

How should students go about answering a tricky question if they have a brain freeze? What steps should they take if the exam paper throws them a curve ball, which can be a scary reality of exam papers? One strategy is to equip learners with a problem-solving approach to apply when they are unsure what steps to take – there are lots of strategies available that can be applied to any type of question, including numeracy-style questions. For example:

- RUCSAC (Read; Underline; Calculation; Solve; Answer; Check)
- UNPACK (Underline keywords; Number the parts of the question; Plan how to answer the question; Answer using specific details; Check your answer; Keep up the great work)
- CUBES (Circle keywords; Underline the question; Box any clue words; Evaluate – what steps do I take?; Solve and check)
- CUSTARD (Circle the command words; Underline other key words; Scribble down points to cover; Think it through; Account for all of the question; Read through your answer; Don't rush or give up).

It can also be worth checking out what problem-solving strategies are being used at feeder primary schools.

Revision books

'Having everything I need in one place keeps me focused.'

If we want children to be successful with their revision, we need to ensure that they are able to revise and that they have everything they need at their fingertips — distilled down for them.

If children are to be successful in maths and with numeracy, they need to spend time deliberately practising. Many schools have introduced slogans to make numeracy a priority for home learning, e.g. #maths30minutesaday and #5mathsQaday. Come up with your own!

Maths, like many subjects, works around core sets of instruction, e.g. rules students must follow in order to solve problems. In maths lessons, students will be introduced to or create methods for solving different problems before applying the method to a range of different questions. There are a range of methods students are introduced to, such as the rules of COSINE, Pythagoras Theorem, procedures for converting numbers into percentages, how to balance equations, and so on. In a typical maths book, a student will write down the 'method' and then spend time practising the steps to complete a series of questions — the difficulty being that the 'how' and relevant instructions can then be lost in the reams of practice. Without the aid of a revision book, it can be quite tricky to locate the method information during revision.

A simple solution to this is to create a revision or reference book in which just key essentials are written so that students are instantly ready for revision. Alongside this book, you could issue students with a jotter-style book for practice. Having all of the key essentials at their fingertips will make revision much easier and give children a go-to guide if they get stuck.

Taking it further

During regular lessons, model using the revision book so that students know how to make the most out of it when they are revising independently.

Bonus idea

Create a guide — 'How to make the most out of your revision book' — for students to stick in the front of their own revision books. Be resolute in how you choose to set these books up, e.g. what should be on the front cover? (Target grade; exam date; marks needed to get to target.) Inside cover? (Guide to using your revision book; a revision checklist; motivational quotes; how to find past papers.) First page? (Tips on effective revision; where and how to get help if they get stuck.)

Numeracy tales

'I hooked them in with a story.'

We have already identified that some students find numeracy tricky – a difficulty that many parents will also share. Where possible, when teaching a mathematical skill or setting a numeracy problem or question, throw in a story to make it interesting and/or relatable for students.

Do explain to students why they need to be able to master a particular numeracy skill and why and how it will be important to them in real life or in later years. Students will always find this more interesting if you also link it to a story. Students are inherently nosey, so you can always use this strategy as an opportunity to build relationships and share a little bit about yourself with your students.

- Tales and stories linked to the news or popular celebrities or sportsmen go down well.
- Use data sets that are of interest to young people – if you are not sure, ask them what things they are interested in.
- If you are dealing with problem-solving questions, use student names if appropriate.
- Personalise stories by providing context and photos to hook students in (see Idea 41).
- If a particular student is struggling with numeracy, find out what things they are into and what they spend their time on outside of school – can you include that kind of stimuli in the story about the numeracy skill or question they are answering?
- Share common problems and successes, e.g. share photos of past student work to tell a story about a common misconception and model this to students at the same time.
- Use objects or props to help to teach maths.

Bonus idea ★

Put a photo of the class through an app such as 'Aging booth' – show what students might look like when they are 30 or 50 years old and relate the maths question to them as an older adult.

Get to grips with a calculator

'I thought it was this scary thing but actually it's quite simple.'

Students are nifty on mobile phones because many use them so often. If we expect students to have the same confidence with calculators, there must be opportunities to use them.

Many subjects, including science, geography, technology, psychology and business, require students to perform calculations – many using a calculator.

- Make a student's calculator part of your routine. When students enter the room, sit down and get their equipment out, make a point of it becoming the expectation that students also put their calculators out on their desks.
- Make it a regular habit of giving students practice of answering questions that require them to use a calculator.
- As with everything, the importance of modelling how to answer questions using a calculator is crucial. If you have a visualiser, model how to answer calculator questions underneath it, being deliberate in your explanation of what to do in a step-by-step approach.
- If calculator questions are a regular feature of your exam, consider laminating a blown-up image of a calculator for reference and use on the wall. For instance, you can use it for modelling or you can get students to use it to demonstrate which functions of the calculator to use and when.
- It can be a good idea to create a 'calculator skills' pack for students – an opportunity just to practise exam questions that require a calculator.

Taking it further

Why not ask a member of the maths department to drop into your lesson to team-teach some of the maths or numeracy skills?

Bonus idea

Do share with members of the maths department any numeracy-style questions and skills required in your exam. Maths staff are a wonderful resource. For example, they might be able to use example geography questions or example data sets as part of their maths lesson. Similarly, the maths department will have a set approach for teaching common numeracy and graph skills, so find out from the experts and use the same approach – it will demonstrate the transfer of skills from one subject to another.

Creative questions

'Making the hard stuff fun brought learning alive for my students.'

Phil Bruce (@pbrucemaths) turns exam questions into creative questions by posing them using everyday objects to spark the interests of learners.

Taking it further

As with wordy maths questions we know that those students who can complete simple arithmetic are at an advantage as, during their exams, they can solve arithmetic questions quickly and therefore gaining time on their peers who may not be as confident. Most schools have TV screens up around school. Why not use these to put up quick-fire questions to enable students to subconsciously practice quick arithmetic, e.g. times tables or addition and subtraction?

Instead of just flashing up the exam question as it would be seen in an exam, use anything available to you (the more creative the better) to pose the exam question. These 'creative questions' can also make for excellent starter activities.

Try setting a creative question in one of these ways:

- Write down the question you want students to answer in an unusual place and take a photograph of it to use back in the classroom. For instance, next time you are on holiday, write a question in the sand on the beach. Next time you are sat in a coffee shop, write a question on a napkin. Students are inherently nosey and this is a great way to capture their imagination.
- Try taking a photo of a question using objects that give clues to the topic or key idea that the question is testing. For instance, for maths you could write a question on a chopped-down tree trunk for logarithms, or for history, write a question on a medicine bottle to link with medicine through time.
- Experiment using everyday objects to create a picture to accompany a question, e.g. creating graphs out of sweets and then posing a question about the graph. This is also a great idea to flip around – get the students to create a graph out of sweets and then ask them the related question.

The possibilities are endless. Creative questions are a fun way to set exam questions and they are a great way to build relationships with classes too.

Give students the list of command words published by your exam board and get them to design their own creative questions about a topic they have been studying. You will be surprised how competitive and imaginative the students get when you introduce the idea of creative questions. Make sure you save any pictures of their creative questions and build up a bank of questions to use over and over again.

Positive maths role models

'Maths is my least favourite subject – I just can't do it!'

Apprehension about maths makes engagement with maths and numeracy questions particularly challenging. The trick is to ensure that maths and numeracy are promoted in a positive light at all times and that, like literacy, everyone considers themselves a teacher of numeracy and talks about maths positively.

Taking it further

Make sure you promote opportunities such as International Maths Day.

Schools should have a clear plan of how to encourage enjoyment of numeracy – from form-time competitive games to promotion of maths quizzes and maths for fun to a programme of enrichment to promote STEM subjects.

If you are teaching numeracy or have mathematical skills to teach as part of your course, ensure you promote enjoyment of these aspects. Even if you are new to teaching numeracy, ensure that you are an advocate of it by promoting the benefits of being numerate at all times. The same goes for TAs.

One of the most powerful things that we can ensure for young people is that they are both literate and numerate before they leave school. Securing the benchmark grade 4 or 5 in these subjects provides a pathway to further education and greater life chances.

Bonus idea ★

Why not suggest delivering a numeracy course for staff? This could be open to anyone or targeted at a particular group of staff, such as TAs, so that they can provide further support to young people and, if needed, small group or one-to-one tuition.

If you're a school leader, do an audit trail. Which staff completed a degree or A level in maths? You will be surprised by the number of staff who have this qualification and it can be a powerful tool knowing that some staff value maths and also have the ability to support the delivery of maths if needed. Don't stop at inside the school gates. Look for good role models who have also been successful in this area and talk to your students about them.

Boosting pupil premium

Part 6

Seating plan

'It's a working document that captures progress made with intervention.'

Seating plans have long been used as tools for managing behaviour and creating the best conditions for learning, e.g. pairing students up for peer mentoring. For many years, Gemma Baxter (@gbaxter_23) has been turning seating plans into a live, working document that can be a crucial tool.

Teaching tip

Ensuring that you know who your pupil premium students are and making their learning and improvement top of your priority list, keeping them fresh in your mind, can only serve to close the gap.

Taking it further

The most functional seating plans will be those where a department works together to share ideas and consider strategies. Suggest to your head of department that your next departmental meeting has a single item agenda: planning intervention based on recent assessment data. Bring your papers to the meeting and discuss common problems and misconceptions, thinking of strategies to move them on.

Bonus idea ★

Try grouping or seating students based on what they can or can't do.

To create your own, print off a copy of your seating plan. Look at the context of your students first, taking into consideration potential barriers to learning. Be sure to highlight pupil premium students on your seating plan to make them stand out rather than labelling this information. This allows you to get to grips with who your key priority groups are. Put the target grade of each student onto the seating plan, along with their most recent assessment score. Focus on the day-to-day data: the tiny steps of progress that are made on a lesson-by-lesson basis. Consider the small detail in their previous assessment that they need to specifically work on to help them make further progress. Once you have diagnosed the problems from the assessment, record the steps and strategies you will take directly onto your seating plan, e.g. 'provide a keywords sheet', 'model exam question structure'. The critical feature of this is that you will see your plan every day and thus your seating plan will serve as a constant reminder every lesson. The best plans are updated regularly after each assessment point, scrapping any strategies that aren't working and trying new ones. Updating the plan can also help affirm what the student needs to do to ensure they are exam-ready. This makes it simple for teachers to keep track of intervention and the progress made towards the exam.

Secure grades

'I know how many marks will get me to the higher grade.'

Incorporate into your marking or reporting a way of showing students how many marks off the next grade they are in the exam. This provides a tangible target and makes targets easy for both parents and students to understand. If marks are too tricky, consider telling students the percentage they are away from the higher grade.

GCSEs have moved from A*–G to 9–1, but how are you letting students know how secure they are in their grade? For instance, a student could be considered a definite grade 5, they may only just be scraping a grade 5, or they may be nearly a grade 6. Teachers must identify where a student lies within these grades. You need to know, students need to know and parents need to know. Determining how secure a student's grade is will allow for effective action-planning, improving student outcomes.

A good starting point for this is the grade boundaries for your subject. Think in terms of the number of marks that separate each grade. Some schools use fine grades, whereby if a student is a secure grade 5, they might be reported as being a grade 5+. Similarly, if their grade was less secure, then the student might be a grade 5= or 5-.

Another helpful way to record progress over time is to record the number of marks students are off the next grade. For instance, if the difference between a grade 4 and 5 is seven marks, you can use this in your calculations of how secure students are in each grade. If a student is a grade 4 but six marks off a grade 5, their fine grade would be grade 4.1.

Teaching tip

Using zero tolerance marking with this strategy is really valuable. Create a slogan for this – such as 'Target is target' – then if a student has failed to reach their target grade, they can see exactly how many marks off it they are and aim to improve their exam by this number of marks. This can be a useful way of tracking progress over time as you can track incremental progress towards grades. It also highlights to students the importance of each and every question and every mark.

Taking it further

This can be a great tool for future exam practices: if a student knows that they are only six marks off the next grade, they could revisit questions trying to scoop up the additional six marks that would take them to a grade 5.

Catwalk books

'I was astonished at what a bit of sticky-back plastic could do!'

How do students know what a great GCSE exercise book looks like? They don't unless you show them.

At the beginning of the course, start by letting students leaf through an older peer's exercise book. Be selective and only model the crème de la crème. This way, the bar for exercise books in terms of layout and organisation is set at a high standard straight away. Get students to carry out their own work scrutiny on model books, identifying good traits in learners.

Ask students the following questions when they start any new exercise book: What will make this book useful for revision? What steps should you take to make sure that this book is easy to revise from? Whenever you get the chance, encourage students to reflect on these questions and consider the presentation of their own notes up to this point.

At checkpoints throughout the year, give students a few minutes to reflect on their organisation and view what their learning looks like in their books. A great way to do this is to carry out a peer book review where students have to mark each other's books and consider how revision-ready each of them are. This can work really well if you teach more than one GCSE class. Swap books between the two and get them to peer mark each other's books. Or if you teach groups across year groups, get your Year 11s to mark your Year 10 group's books. This is a great exercise for students as it gives them the opportunity to revisit prior learning but in a much more novel way, as most students love to mark other students' books... if only they knew!

Past students

'When I saw what he had achieved, it made me believe I could have the same life.'

Use past students as a motivator and share their ideas and top tips with students in the run-up to exams.

For a long time in my gym there was a sign up saying 'it's only difficult until it's easy'. I'm not a big gym-goer, but this quote is sometimes just enough for me to get on a treadmill. The quote wasn't from a Photoshopped celebrity with a secret personal trainer; it was from a member of the gym – someone who, like me, possibly just wants to be able to eat more. There is power in being motivated by peers – people who have travelled along the same road.

Schools should work hard to keep in touch with past students. Most universities have an alumni association and regularly get in touch to find out what past students are up to and where they've ended up. This is something you can tap into. Get photos and quotes or exam tips from past students who achieved a range of different grades so that there is someone that every student can relate to. Include what grade they got in their final exam, what doors opened for them as a result and details of where they are now and what career they hope to go on to.

If you can, arrange for past students to come in and contribute to an assembly about steps students should be taking to be revision- and exam-ready. Get them to outline what they did in the run-up to their exams and what they did that helped them to get their grade, along with their ideas and tips for what they wished they'd done differently.

Taking it further

Instead of paying external companies, get past students in to run workshops for students on 'How to revise'.

Bonus idea ★

On results day, take a video recorder and get students on the spot to say what made a difference to them. This can also be a great way to get students to say a big thank you to their teachers. Play it on the first staff training day back after the summer holidays as a motivator.

Are they getting it?

'My lessons might go swimmingly but how can I tell if learners are actually getting it?'

The most effective teachers will build a series of learning checks into their lessons to ensure that learners are actually understanding the content. While probing questioning can be great, it can be time-consuming. If you have a class of 30 students, the task of asking each and every student an individual probing question is not feasible.

Teaching tip

If a student has proven they can do something and have understood the learning, great! This is an indicator that they are ready to move on or try out their learning within a different context. If, however, students haven't understood it, this must be picked up and acted upon as soon as possible. There may be opportunities for peer teaching here – for instance, if some students have grasped concepts and others are still struggling, pair them up.

Dylan Wiliam provides a great tool in his concept of hinge questions – a point in the lesson when you need to diagnose whether or not all students are ready to move on with their learning. (You can hear more about hinge questions from Dylan Wiliam here: www.youtube.com/watch?v=Mh5SZZt207k.) These types of questions get a response from every student in the class that then gives you the evidence of what your students can or can't do – allowing you to plan the right next move with your teaching. But what else can you do to check student progress instantly throughout the lesson? Here are a few ideas to try:

- Give each student a whiteboard for writing down answers to questions.
- Give students A, B, C cards to hold up. Give them a hinge question to answer.
- After talking through a key idea, give students a short amount of time to write down the main points you have said or to write a summary.
- Give students a quick-fire round of true or false, or set a quick quiz to check they have been listening. This doesn't always have to be written down; they could verbally answer these questions in pairs.
- Get students to explain what they have just learnt to a friend and then get their friends to

Taking it further

Consider implementing strategies such as a ten-minute takeover (Idea 75).

feed back (a checklist of things peers can tick off is great for this).

- Get students to draw a picture to show their learning.
- Give students a cloze test based on their learning.
- Get students to shrink down their learning onto a sticky note.
- Get students to pick out points from their learning that could help them to answer a particular exam question.
- Give students a dummy answer and ask them to spot the mistakes.
- Give students a half-baked exam answer to finish off. Be creative in your presentation of this – perhaps someone has spilled their drink over half of the answer and students have to fill it in.
- Give students an answer without the question. Get students to guess the question and how many marks it got.
- Get students to make a list of five key ideas or get them to draw round their hand and jot down five things they have learnt.
- Provide students with an answer. Make students read through it and highlight all the examples used. Task students with the challenge of thinking of extra examples or better examples that they could use instead.
- Write an answer out in front of students but make some deliberate mistakes – get students to make a note of any corrections they would make to your answer.
- Get students to complete a comic strip to show their learning. A quick way to do this is to give them a completed cartoon drawing and ask them to fill out what the cartoon is saying.
- Give students a series of checkpoint questions to answer. The outcome from these can determine the next steps of the lesson.

These activities are only as useful as what you do with the outcome. It is equally important to know what students can do as well as what they can't do.

Bonus idea ★

Get a set of red, amber and green book boxes for your classroom. Give students the task of self-assessing their own understanding of the lesson on the way out of the door. Students drop their book into the box that best suits their learning: green if they've grasped it and could explain their learning to a Year 10; amber if they have understood it but would need their notes to explain what they have learnt; red if they still have questions or are unsure.

Live mark

'Motivational, meaningful and manageable!'

Some of the most effective ideas are not necessarily new ones. It is important that we work out what is working and what isn't, so we can invest time in something that is actually going to make a difference. Live marking makes a difference – it provides timely feedback that can be motivational!

The idea behind live marking is that students get feedback almost instantly, and actually this is easier to achieve that you think. The first principle is that you have to opt in. Don't sit down at all. Carry a pen with you at all times. Read work as you circulate the room (even if it is just a paragraph). Alternatively, use a whiteboard pen to mark student desks, e.g. a tick if the student is doing what you expect, double tick if they are exceeding expectations, numbers if you see an area for improvement – you could have the corresponding guidance on the board so students can see how to self-correct.

Jotting down feedback on a sticky note can work in the same way – have these pre-typed or written out so that you can simply go and drop these onto a student's desk while they are working. Or give students a shopping list of success criteria to meet – you or they can tick it off as you see it in their work.

Motivate students by linking your live marking to rewards, e.g. achievement points or merits. Pre-print these onto reusable cards and place them onto student desks to show when and where they have been rewarded for excellence. Similarly, have every student with their planner open on their desk – jot down notes for parents to see. All of these strategies can be done by the teacher, TA or peers but they all mean that feedback is instant and timely.

Revision workshops

'Exams were very different in my day!'

For most students, if they break up for study leave, that's it — the cord is cut. It's over to the student to uphold their end of the bargain and revise. Parents and guardians are there for the ride, too. Parents are equal partners but how can they be expected to help their children revise if they don't know how to revise themselves? This may be especially relevant to pupil premium students — equipping their guardians with such knowledge might be the key to greater pupil and parent buy-in.

In one way or another, information on how to revise needs to make it home so that parents can make a difference. Parents need to have explicit detail on how their children should be revising for each of their subjects because one size does not fit all. If you can, send home a revision guide or hand one out at parents' evening. Sometimes the best way to know how to do something effectively is going through the motions.

Organise a 'How to revise workshop' for parents and students. Invite them along to attend a series of seminars. Get the best practitioners in the school to run sessions to upskill parents in things such as: methods of active revision; how to support anxious students; how to summarise notes; how to go about creating revision materials such as mind maps and flash cards; how to use them for low-stakes testing; how students should be preparing for their exams; how to use technology such as mobiles tablets as part of a revision strategy; and how to mark past papers. On the same night, teachers who are not running sessions could book appointments to speak to parents and students, particularly those who might need a little extra guidance or students who must take some extra steps to secure progress.

Teaching tip

Why not give parents a copy of their child's exam timetable too? Get them to sit down with their child to plan out revision time, explaining the importance of spacing and revisiting content.

Taking it further

If you are having difficulties getting parents to attend, find out why – do they work shifts? Are they receiving the information from school? Can they read information from school? Remove as many barriers as possible. Consider offering dinner as part of the workshops – this might improve attendance to key events.

Bonus idea ★

Set up a revision shop to sell everything that a student might need, from revision guides to exam-ready pencil cases.

Exam traps

'One of the best ways for students to learn is through mistakes.'

A mistake is only a mistake if students don't learn from it. Modelling common misconceptions can help students avoid repeating the same slip-ups in their real exam. Helping students deal with their own mistakes can ensure that they aid progress, rather than hinder it. As a teacher, understanding why students are making the same mistakes will help to improve your teaching.

Avoiding common pitfalls in the exam is vital for students. Every year, each exam board publishes an examiner's report, which outlines the most common errors candidates made. You will probably have read it but have you built the outcomes of it into your lessons? Students enjoy trying to anticipate 'common mistakes' or looking at work to 'spot the mistake' that others have made.

There are many ways that mistakes can be modelled – from the most basic 'WWW – What Went Wrong' starter activities to more complex or subtle misunderstandings in longer-answer questions. Regular exposure to exam-style questions and incorrect answers can help students feel more confident and avoid errors. The focus of the mistakes could change from a literacy (SPaG) focus, to content, numeracy or graph skills. Here are some ideas to try:

- GCSE question and answer – ask students to 'predict the most common mistake' (instead of them actually writing an answer).
- Give students a completed answer to a question and challenge them to find five literacy mistakes in it or three things they would add in to improve it.
- Students can be the teacher for a topic in groups or as a class and mark previous or classmates' answers, focusing on any errors.

They don't even need to give it a score – the feedback alone is enough.

- You can get students to complete assessments without a grade or score, instead focusing on any mistakes they made and how to put them right. Too often students focus on the number or score rather than how to improve, which is the main aim of internal assessments and mock exams.
- You can place the focus on the use of keywords by comparing two answers – both covering the same point but one including keywords and the other more basic language. They can display to students what their answers are missing (rather than just what they should look like).
- Using different coloured highlighters, students can highlight parts of an answer that are correct and then, in a different colour, any parts of the answer that are incorrect or irrelevant to the question.
- Class-sharing of mistakes helps students to realise that it is okay to make them, as long as they can learn from them. You could try encouraging students to model their mistakes and how they are going to avoid them now they know.
- Use examiners' reports to look through previous tests as a class. Discuss how to avoid the errors or why students made them.
- Use as a starter or plenary the question, 'What's the biggest mistake with this answer?'.
- Create a fail wall in your classroom and celebrate learning from mistakes.

Taking it further

The competition that comes with trying to 'spot the mistake' or 'predict the common misconception' can engage students and make them think carefully about a question before rushing to answer it. Sharing mistakes also reduces the significance of future errors, meaning students are more open and more likely to learn!

Bonus idea

Most exam boards now have a tool where you can see how students have done and what mark they achieved for each individual question. Use this information to find out where last year's cohort lost marks and then take the steps to avoid this happening again.

Explain your brain

'How would you answer that question?'

The Sutton Trust-EEF Teaching and Learning Toolkit (see Idea 10) shows us that metacognition has a huge impact on learning progress. Never has it been so beneficial to ensure that you are deliberate in the practice of modelling your thought processes. The importance of modelling per question or for an entire exam cannot be underestimated for all students, but especially for those pupils who may not benefit from having help from parents with revision.

We know that high-quality teacher instruction can reap huge benefits and this also applies to how you instruct students to tackle a question or exam. For each exam and type of exam question, instruct students on how you would approach each question, explaining and modelling every step as you do it. Be sure to explain to students your thinking – on reading and interpreting an exam question, and step-by-step instruction on how to answer and self-check for accuracy. At every stage, be sure to remind students of what they should be considering.

There are many ways to model your thinking – especially when applying this to exam practice. Model to students how you would answer one question or a whole exam paper from start to finish. Get students to copy out what you do or create a cheat sheet based on your modelling of how to tackle an exam question. Get students to re-enact the process for their peers e.g. model their thinking out loud as they answer a similar exam question, or write their top tips for answering a certain style of exam question. Students can take away the same exam question you completed in front of them for homework or complete this same question at the start of the following lesson.

Taking it further

After modelling how to answer a question once, on the next practice prompt students with what they should be doing and when – you could even set this up on a PowerPoint™ against a timer. This could then be a great tool for students to also reuse at home.

Bonus idea ★

After modelling how to answer a question, always give students the opportunity to have a go themselves on the next practice and review what they have learnt from your demonstrations. Try a quick quiz based on your instructions. Always make sure students are clear on how valuable this practice is, e.g. by asking them to share two things they have learnt today that will help them in the exam.

Exam focus

'I can't believe that I didn't prioritise this already!'

Make sure you put an 'exam focus' into every one of your lessons. Better still, include one in every activity.

There's no escaping it. You earn your crust by how well your students perform in their exam(s). Therefore, it is common sense to immerse students in as many example questions and/or specimen papers as possible. The more exposure students get to the exam and its contents, the more familiar they will be with its structure, layout and style and the better placed students will be to achieve success. As a rule of thumb, put at least one exam focus into every lesson – more than one if the knowledge or skill being learnt allows it.

- Use potential exam questions or command words as part of your goals or aims for lessons (see Idea 33).
- Show how the content of the lesson could appear in their exam.
- Build in explicit opportunities for students to complete an actual exam question, using a mark scheme or even getting students to self-assess their confidence levels in answering a question.
- Look at the materials your exam board has to offer. Is an examiner's report useful for students to read and then act upon?
- Could students spend time designing their own exam questions based on key ideas from the specification, or keep a list of rubric errors to avoid?
- Could you include a method of active revision in your lesson? Is there a way of revisiting past topics in your lessons, emulating what students will have to do once they start their study leave?

Teaching tip

Could you start the lesson by giving everyone an example front cover from an exam so that each student is familiar with its layout and any instructions provided by the exam board? Get them to practise filling one out.

Bonus idea ★

Be sure not to just focus on using past paper questions, as the likelihood of these ever being reused by the exam board is minimal. Get a group of teachers together and come up with a bank of potential questions. Make sure these are derived from the wording presented in the exam specification. It is a great idea to double-check the list of command words linked to your specification (there is usually a list you can download from each exam board) and use these regularly in practice questions.

Effort equals progress

'This is a great idea for rewarding students who work hard but sometimes get missed.'

Reward effort over ability. Effort is the thing that will make the difference in exam outcomes.

Teaching tip

Performance tables aside, as teachers we have a moral obligation to try to give every student in our care the best possible start for the next stage in their life – check out the Pygmalion Effect. You can find an excellent video about it here: www.youtube.com/ watch?v=hTghEXKNj 7g&t=47s

Bonus idea ★

It is important to highlight achievement. If a student's target grade is a 5 and on previous pieces of work they managed to score a grade 3, they could be considered to be making below-expected progress. But if on a follow-up exercise they go on to secure a grade 5 – a difference of two grades – they would be making expected progress. Turn such things into an achievement league table. Put students with above-expected progress high up on the board.

Unless you are comment-only marking, when students get a piece of work returned that's been teacher-assessed, there is always a scramble of students checking for the grade they have achieved. But what if a student is one of the weaker-ability students in your class, whose target grade is a 4 but who, as yet, hasn't managed to scrape it? Then imagine if this same student is a grade 4 or below in every one of their subjects. This student might bounce from one classroom to the next all day, being told that their performance is not good enough, knowing that their performance is not going to secure them a place at college or on an apprenticeship.

Changes in school performance measures, and the introduction of initiatives such as the English Baccalaureate, have meant that the make-up of some classes has changed dramatically over the last five years, especially as some qualifications no longer count towards accountability measures. This means that, in all likelihood, you are faced with the challenge of teaching students who would really be better placed in alternative provision. How do you make students who aren't scraping the required pass grades motivated? How can you make their performance meaningful in comparison to other students in the same class who might regularly be achieving top grades? The answer lies not in assessing grades but instead in measuring progress based on effort.

Revisit

'A student who never forgets doesn't exist!'

Revisiting things they have previously learnt is a great way to make sure that students don't forget them! One way is to set up an activity that makes students skim over their notes.

On an A3 piece of paper, get students to mind-map the keywords, ideas or themes of a topic or module. Then get students to annotate each keyword, idea or theme using any information they can remember. Encourage them to try to come up with connections between the key ideas or themes by drawing lines between them and writing the thing that connects the ideas along the line. Once students have completed this from memory, give them the chance to delve back into their notes, topping up their piece of work with any ideas they might have missed. They could do this in a different-coloured pen to make it stand out to them in future. Finally, issue students with an ultimate teacher checklist of things they should have included on their piece of work, before giving them the opportunity to consolidate their learning by answering an example question. Plan your questioning so that it layers up the activity. For instance, once students have completed it without looking back in their books, have them return to it and define all of the key terms they have used. Or get them to write on facts that might be linked to any of the key ideas around them. Around the outside of their work, they could write example questions that might rely on this learning, or key summary points. If you have completed the course, get different groups of students to do this activity for the different units of work, before moving each topic to other groups to add more information.

Teaching tip

Why not get students to make a giant version of this to go on the wall or let them draw it out on classroom tables with whiteboard pens? Or invest in a roll of cheap wallpaper and use this to create a revision wall that students can write revision notes on.

Taking it further

Be sure to relate this learning to the exam and ask students what they will need this knowledge for in the exam. For instance, what section of the exam will this content be needed for?

Bonus idea ★

Get students to keep a revision log to record any revision or revisiting of topics they do in lessons or at home. This will help students to identify the parts of the specification they haven't yet revised.

Skill improvement

'The tally chart proved to me that we were covering the right stuff.'

You must have ways to ensure that you can assess how your students' skills are improving over time. One way of doing this is to give each student a checklist of skills they must be competent in demonstrating.

Teaching tip

Where possible after students have practised a skill (e.g. drawing a composite bar chart), they should be given an additional opportunity to practise the skill but in a different context. This gives them the chance to act on any feedback immediately. A good strategy is to revisit any skills taught in lessons immediately through a piece of homework. This gives students an additional opportunity to immediately consolidate their learning.

Taking it further

You could keep a copy of the checklist in your planner too, so you know how many times students have practised each of the different skills.

Bonus idea ★

Examples of exam skills can be another useful display to put up, along with a 'how to' guide.

Exams are made up of questions that challenge students' knowledge *and* skills. For some subjects, there will even be explicit questions that expect students to showcase a particular skill.

Create a tally chart of all the skills required for the exam and ask students to tally when they practise each skill as you go through the course. This can also act as a self-assessment tool, where students can rate their confidence level for each skill. A sample skill tally is provided in the online resources for this book.

Every time a skill is practised by a student, you must make sure you have built in some way of assessing to what degree they have mastered it. Build time in your planning to address misconceptions and provide extra practice. The number and type of skills expected by the exam board will determine the number of opportunities for practice. For instance, a typical geography specification has in excess of 40 skills that students could be examined on. As a rule of thumb, aim to visit each skill at least five times in class, through practice exam questions or homework pieces.

It can help to pinpoint in students' exercise books each time a skill has been practised – sticky index tabs are great for this. Each time a student practises a skill, they should check the feedback from their last practice so they can act on it and keep improving.

Target test

'She kept forgetting where her focus should be.'

All too often, students will skip to the grade or mark you have awarded them for a question. They pay lip service to your carefully thought-out handwritten comments. Use this strategy to check that students know what they ought to be acting on lesson by lesson.

A straightforward strategy is to test students on their targets. At the start of a lesson, give each student a sticky note. Put up a slide on the board announcing that in a few minutes everyone will be sitting a test. Reassure students that there is no need to revise.

Make sure all exercise books or marked past papers are out of reach and lay down the question: 'What do you need to do to be better in this subject?' You might even put this question into context: if they have recently sat a test or past paper, ask, 'What target did I give you on your last eight-mark question?' Students should write their responses on a sticky note. Give them a couple of minutes to dwell on their areas for self-improvement before letting them self-assess their responses using their own exercise books or whatever piece of work you marked last to check whether they got it right.

This activity is very powerful. First, it forces students to think about the feedback you have given them. Second, it gives them space to reflect on their targets and show their understanding of your feedback, as they have to summarise it in their own words. It is a good way to see whether they actually understand what they have to do to improve. It gives students who can't answer the posed question a sharp reminder of the importance of taking on board your comments.

Teaching tip

Later in this book there are strategies you can employ to help keep any targets for action alive, both during the lesson and for future exam practice.

Taking it further

Follow up this activity with an opportunity for students to act on the feedback or to practise whatever it is that will make them better in your subject. Alternatively, give them a bit of time to write down a couple of steps or actions that they are going to take to meet the targets you have set them.

Supporting SEND students

Part 7

Making the most of your TA

'We're in it together!'

Teaching assistants can add incredible value to the progress of your class if they are used effectively. Some slight tweaks in your relationship with your TA can be of benefit to your class.

Taking it further

Always check that your TA is encouraging students to tackle tasks independently before providing support.

In order for you to make the most out of your teaching assistant, they need the heads-up as to what lessons are coming up and, more importantly, what knowledge and skills are going to be taught and how they can help students. If you have ever taught a cover lesson, you will know the feeling of walking into a room and only finding out from reading the cover work on the desk what you have to teach – it's not conducive to great levels of progress and if a TA isn't familiar with the content being covered, it can limit the amount of support they can provide. As a bare minimum you should make sure you provide your TA with:

1. A class seating plan.
2. Class data sheet – including details of students' target grades and current grade – which will enable your TA to also target additional support to other students.
3. Details of students' strengths and weaknesses.
4. A copy of the relevant textbook and revision book.
5. The scheme of learning, including where they could access lesson-by-lesson resources if they have the time to view them.
6. A few top tips on what else you would like their support with. This is particularly important, as most TAs won't want to 'tread on your toes'.

Here is a list of things you may want to suggest to your TA they could help you with:

- Circulating the room and checking for SPGST errors – live marking as they roam.
- Checking that students are on-task and prompting any students who are not.
- Praising students for effort.
- Encouraging students to take on extra challenge tasks if they see a student has completed a task.
- Regularly checking that student books are organised.
- Checking student planners to ensure they have recorded homework correctly.
- Checking revision resources.
- Double-checking books of key students.
- Keeping an exercise book themselves, providing work for any students who are absent from a particular lesson.
- Keeping a note and regularly sharing with you concerns of things that students seem to 'not be getting' or students who they feel aren't working hard enough.
- Collecting examples of great work to use for modelling – if you have a school camera, equip your TA with it during a lesson to snap great work or examples of great answers (see Idea 17).
- Most importantly, ask your TA whether there is anything else they would like to support you with. Have you missed any potential marginal gains with your students?
- Invite your TA to attend any revision sessions you run – they could just be free to attend and support.

Like for like

'Practising helped me to feel comfortable with the scribe before the real thing.'

For final exams, some students will have a reader, others may have a scribe, a few children may have both and some may even be completing their exam on a laptop. The more experience and practice these students have with this layer of support, the better adapted they will be. The same goes for students who are permitted extra time in the exam. A very powerful thing you can do is to make sure you write down details of any exam concessions on your seating plans so that you know what they are.

Quite simply, if a student has a concession (any one of the above allowances), then make sure they have that concession available for every mock exam and every practice question you get them to complete. If you have a TA in your lesson, get their help with this. If you know you are getting students to complete exam practice during a lesson, see whether it is possible to plan for adding in the relevant concessions. For example, if a student is going to be sitting their exams and typing out their answers onto a laptop, the more practice they get at this, the quicker they are likely to be able to type and the more comfortable they will be typing out their answers and also self-checking answers on a laptop, opposed to on a piece of paper. The same goes for students permitted a scribe. It is one thing reading through and checking an answer that has been written in your own handwriting – it is a completely different task reading an answer you have spoken out aloud that someone else has then written down.

Kid speak

'Why can't they just say it as it is? Why can't they just put it in kid speak?' (Year 11 student on exam questions)

One of the things students can find hard is deciphering what exam questions are actually asking them to do. A powerful strategy to help students manoeuvre their way around tricky exam questions is to teach them how to translate exam questions into 'kid speak'.

Spending time breaking questions down into a series of instructions ensures that all students can fully comprehend questions and respond to them correctly. Following the steps below helps students understand what examiners are looking for.

1 Introduce the exam question to the students and get them to highlight the command words: '**Explain** the ways in which a coastal environment is managed to guarantee it is conserved, but used sustainably.' Understanding command words is key to understanding what the examiner wants.
2 Students should then be looking to interpret the remainder of the question and create themselves a set of instructions. Using the term 'instructions' can really help students to generate an accurate interpretation of exactly what they have to do. For this example, students should:
    a. refer to a coastal environment they have learnt about, e.g. a sand dune
    b. explain how the area is conserved but used sustainably.

After modelling this process to students a few times, they should automatically start to take this approach when tackling questions. It will make them feel more confident (especially those of weaker ability) in knowing exactly what the examiner is looking for.

Teaching tip

The examiner uses the concept of a 'command word'. In kid speak this translates to a 'demand word'.

Taking it further

Reverse it. Give students an exam question in kid speak and get them to practise putting it into examiner speak.

Bonus idea ★

There are lots of strategies out there to help students deconstruct questions; one handy one to try is agreement circles. After setting an exam question, get students to draw a circle in their book. Around the outside they should each write down things they would include in their answer. Next, working with peers, students should share their ideas and write the best ones inside the circle.

Learning speeds

'Some students grasp difficult concepts with ease and other learners need longer to get to grips with challenging ideas.'

Most teachers under the pressure of teaching for a test will hold the reins of each learning experience to a strangulating degree, but learning gains can be secured by engaging students to make decisions about their own learning. Consider trying one or more of the following activities to engage your learners.

Think about a typical lesson in your classroom: do you move every learner through the lesson at the same pace or do you let students set their own learning speed? Are the skills and level of challenge set at the right pace for your learners? How are you ensuring you are getting the most out of your students? How do you plan to prevent passive learners from coasting along? There are different ways teachers can differentiate learning for students; these might be through the end product of a lesson or learning episode, by task, through intervention or by allowing students to take different journeys through their learning.

- A great way to identify and start to plan your class's learning journey can be to give students a progress and intervention checklist (Idea 71) and get them to rate their existing knowledge and skills as red, amber or green (RAG) before doing any learning. This information can then be used to plan the lessons from here on in.
- In a lesson, set completely different tasks. All students can work on the same learning goal, but provide them with a choice of activities. For example, you could set five tables with five different activities students can opt for.
- them to collect as many points as they can.
- Give students a choice over the journey they take during a lesson. Give students freedom to choose, where possible, what to investigate

and how to study in order to increase their interest in learning. Or set up a different number of steps to reach an end goal. Give students choice over which steps they take.

- Differentiate through the instructions you give students. For instance, below grade 4 learners might need visual clues or benefit from graphic organisers, scaffolding or pre-teaching vocabulary.
- Create activities that are open-ended, so they either have no limit to challenge or are open activities for which there is no predetermined right answer.
- Use pace and variety: use rapid pacing, where appropriate, in presenting new material and use a variety of methods to maintain student interest and accommodate different learning styles.
- Make your tasks get progressively difficult and set different starting points for students.
- Get every student in your class to write their name onto a sticky note. Project on the board an arrow continuum entitled 'Are you making progress?' The start of the arrow should represent the lowest GCSE grade and the arrow head (pointy bit) the highest GCSE grade. Annotate the length of the arrow with statements linked to the learning, recognising what is required to achieve each GCSE grade. At critical points during the lesson, get students to position a sticky note with their name on along the continuum to indicate the progress they are making during the lesson. Allow students to work their way along the continuum at their own pace.
- Create a series of GCSE questions and set them out in the formation of a pyramid made out of blocks. Write a question for students to answer on each block. At the base of the pyramid, the questions should be easy and typical questions a grade 4 student should be able to answer. The higher up the pyramid, the harder the questions should become, with one grade 9 question on the top. Let students pick where they start on the pyramid.

Flip it out

'This is a novel way of putting something right in someone's face every lesson.'

Decide what information students would benefit from having in front of them every lesson and consolidate it into a page that can be flipped out of their books.

Print out whatever it is that would help students, e.g. a list of command words and their definitions. Make sure the orientation is the same style as your students' exercise books. Trim it down so that it fits into an exercise book. Leave a flap on the left edge of the sheet. As it faces you, put a line of glue along the back left-hand edge of the piece of paper and then get students to stick it onto the edge of the back inside cover of their exercise book. Ta-dah! Whenever you want students to look at the key information, they can just flip it out. It can be out on the table while they are working in order for them to use it for reference.

Flip outs are great for a multitude of things. At Key Stage 3, you could use them to record teacher marking comments that students should be consciously acting on while completing new pieces of work.

At Key Stage 4, a better use of a flip out could be for a list of specialist terms that students should be using where possible in their work.

It could also be used as a reminder tool for how to respond to questions, e.g. the rules for responding to 12-mark questions, or it could be used to provide students with support tools such as sentence starters.

Functional displays

'Picturing where the display was in the classroom helped me to remember what was on the poster.'

The idea is very simple. Create a display based on the likely command words that could come up in exams. Put up a display in a position where it will be functional in your lessons.

There is nothing worse than students losing marks in their exam for rubric errors such as misinterpreting the exam question. Some students have a habit of spilling out everything they know and still not answering the actual question. The reason this can happen is down to students not being familiar with the command words used in exam questions. If you put 'exam command words' into a search engine, there are a range of pre-made slides filled with the definitions and ready to use. If you haven't already got a keywords display up, take some time to put one up in your classroom. This can be one of the most important and useful displays you have, so make sure it doesn't get swallowed up in your room.

- If you are going to invest your time in something, you need to make it pay for itself. Use it. Build its use into lessons from Key Stage 3, not just exam classes.
- When introducing your lesson goal or learning objectives, get students to show their understanding of each aim by unpicking its meaning using your command word display (Idea 33).
- In your exam classes, make students decode different exam questions using the definitions on your wall.
- While teaching or practising exam questions, actively refer to your wall.
- Get students to write their own exam questions based on the types of command words they might encounter in their exam.

Teaching tip

Students could pick the exam command words they find most tricky from the display and then answer example questions.

Taking it further

Plaster up example exams for the matching command word. Or why not flip the idea and give students a completed answer for which they have to guess the command word the answer is responding to?

Bonus idea ★

If you don't have a classroom of your own, turn this idea into a command word literacy mat. Get a set laminated and keep them close to hand as a tool for students to refer to when looking at exam questions.

Pushing gifted and higher students – developing independence

Part 8

Exam conference

'The best lesson ever. This is the happiest I have ever been at school.'

One of the things that can reignite passive students and spur them into action is the element of surprise. It keeps students on their toes and can force them to re-engage with learning. There are a variety of ways you can surprise your students. One of my favourites is to organise an exam conference.

On arrival to what would be their normal lesson, stand at the doorway of your classroom and welcome students to the exam conference. If you've attended any run-of-the-mill training courses, you will be familiar with how they start – treat your lesson in the same way. If you can, set up your classroom like a conference, moving your tables into small groups or a large discussion table. Consider ring-fencing the first ten minutes of your lesson for networking and arrange for tea and coffee for your students. As a one-off, this can be really powerful and a great way of showing your students that you care. It can double-up as a treat lesson, too.

During the lesson, get students to work together on different activities, e.g. revisiting learning in a group, or designing an exam question and mark scheme based on their prior learning.

Running an exam conference is one way to shock your learners into action. But there are other things you can organise to get your most passive learners involved. Here are a few:

- If you have a double lesson, let your class have a short learning break. This can re-energise students. Give them a couple of minutes to pop to the toilet or grab a breath of fresh air. Be clear that anyone who takes liberties won't be allowed a learning break in the future.

- Change the location of your lesson. Take students into a different classroom or into the library or hall as a one-off. If permitted, consider taking your class outside.
- Invite a different teacher to take the lesson or team-teach a lesson.
- Sneak the element of surprise into your lesson. For instance, hide things for students to find. This could be sticking a worksheet or exam question under a student's chair or hiding a secret message somewhere in their books for them to discover.
- Create activities that require students to get up out of their chairs, e.g. to read information around the room before transforming it into something else.
- Make it compulsory to work with a variety of people during the lesson.
- Incorporate activities such as speed dating or quiz trade, or scatter information among different students to share.
- If your classroom is big enough and tidy enough, hide stuff for students to find.
- Mix up your seating plan regularly to keep students on their toes.
- Use music to liven up an activity or use a tune as a timer. Let students nominate songs to play.
- Design a board game using exam questions for students to play.
- Chop a model answer up into sentences or single words and get students to work together to put it back together again.
- Give students a model answer with some of the words or phrases blacked out. Students could work together to guess the parts of the answer that are hidden.

> **Bonus idea** ★
>
> As a teacher, one of the biggest decisions can be how to position students' desks. Try having them set up in rows facing the board with space between each of the desks. This allows you to easily chat to a student sitting on either side of the desk, and at a second's notice you can also turn them into groups of tables by pushing three together.

Super-challenge

'I competed with my mates to see who could finish the most super-challenges.'

Extension tasks have been the norm for a long time, but do they really push a student into giving their absolute best? What kind of incentive does being handed more work give to a student who has completed the original task? Why not replace the term 'extension task' and instead provide students with the opportunity to choose to complete either a 'challenge task' or a 'super-challenge task'?

For a long time in GCSEs, we have used the term 'A* challenge'. The new wave of grades 1–9 means that this is no longer relevant. 'Grade 9 challenge' doesn't mean anything to students yet, so in the interim we have moved to encouraging students to complete 'super-challenge tasks'. This is a concept that can also be applied in Key Stage 3.

When setting work, the main task should require students to push themselves to grade 9 standard. The challenge and super-challenge needn't be more of the same but instead an opportunity for students to further their thinking or learning in a way that is linked to an additional skill rather than just more work. Or it could provide an opportunity to deliberately practise what they have learnt in a way that will enhance their exam performance.

For instance, if a student has been working towards creating an answer to 'Describe the responses to a tsunami' and has finished their answer ahead of time and before their classmates, this student must then be pushed to apply their thinking further through either a challenge or an even more testing super-challenge. These should not simply be more of the same activity but instead an activity that deepens their knowledge or skill. Sticking with the example of a tsunami, a challenge task could be for students to create their own exam question about tsunamis using the relevant section of the exam specification. This forces students to do something different using their learning, with the added incentive that it doesn't require the student to write reams and reams of more work. If posed correctly, the student will have to revisit their notes on tsunamis, consider the knowledge they have learnt and then think about the range of command words that could be applied to the knowledge. You may then also push the student to rank the possible exam questions they have generated, based on how confident they would feel in answering them or from easiest to toughest. A super-challenge could then be for them to think about the questions they have generated and put them into a sequence as they might appear in an actual exam. For instance, most exams chunk questions on a similar theme. This is useful to a student as when they come to revise, they have a bank of ready-made practice questions. Remember that these are better than past papers as the same questions are unlikely to reappear!

> **Bonus idea**
>
> Include layered challenges on homework tasks too.

Pick out the grade 9

'I wanted to collect them all.'

Sometimes a tick just won't cut it. Devise a way of rewarding and picking out the grade 9 or A* elements in student responses to exam answers.

Grade 9 or A* stickers can be a real treat for students. If school funds are tight, make your own line of stickers to recognise grade 9 traits in answers. These can be especially useful if students are struggling with a high-end exam skill such as 'demonstrating reasoned evaluation' in geography or 'justifications made with specific reasoned conclusions' in PE. Try creating stickers for all grades, e.g. 'Grade 9 explanation – out of this world!' and 'Great use of specialist terms! Grade 3 SPGST'.

Stickers can be great way of building exam question self-confidence in students. For example, a grade 4 candidate might not be able to produce a complete grade 9 answer but elements of their work may be of this standard and stickers like these can be great for recognising this. They can be really powerful for engaging disaffected students, as praise is often showered on the most able. Highlighting areas of their answers that are great will indicate to students that they should repeat and develop these areas in their answers in future exam practices too.

Practice links

'This can become an unconscious skill.'

Students often struggle with applying the correct knowledge to questions. Opportunities for practising could be created in lessons to avoid common problems that cost students marks.

Two years' worth of content is usually examined over just a couple of hours – wow! One of the things teachers must be confident about is knowing that a candidate can match the appropriate knowledge or skill to the right question.

Practising the meaning of command words is helpful, but students need deliberate practice in knowing how to select the content that should go with a particular question. This is especially useful in literacy-based subjects such as English or the humanities.

Where possible, create the opportunity for students to practise allocating content to past exam questions. For instance, in history give students a whole past paper along with the task of jotting down the knowledge they would need to include in their answers. After they have linked the knowledge needed for each question, they could go on to answer them. If students struggle with picking out the correct content to include in their answers or they are getting muddled up, consider giving them a paired activity whereby the task is to match the question with the content.

Taking it further

Don't forget to read examiners' reports and ensure you are covering common mistakes that students regularly make in your teaching of knowledge or skills.

Bonus idea

Another way to encourage students to link their learning to exam questions is to allow students to make the mistake. Then re-teach to avoid the same mistakes happening in the real exam!

Target practice

'It's a constant reminder of what I need to do to be better.'

The idea of using a bookmark to record a feedforward target is straightforward and effective. A feedforward target is something that students carry over and act on to improve their performance in future exam practices and should be recorded on a bookmark.

Teaching tip

Build 'target time' into lessons. Hand over some time to students to refocus on their targets and consider whether they have achieved them. Why not get students to highlight evidence of where they have acted on their feedforward target in their book or in an exam paper?

Taking it further

Consider including a photo of the student on their bookmark. This idea makes students much less likely to lose their bookmark and makes it truly theirs. Even better, take a photo of each student holding up their target grade on a mini-whiteboard. This will help to keep the bigger picture of a great exam result central to their mind.

Teachers spend copious amounts of time providing students with written comments on answers to exam questions. A huge amount of time is then invested in getting students into the habit of responding to these written comments and, in most instances, this cycle secures improvement. But then what? When is this advice ever returned to? After responding to and acting on feedback comments, do learners actually understand what they did? Can they transfer the knowledge of how they improved their exam question to a completely dissimilar question or to a question that is on a totally different topic? Do they know what they have to do to continue to get better? How can teachers keep these targets for learning as action points for learning rather than just comments stuck on static pieces of work? One solution is to use a bookmark.

Using a bookmark as part of a sequence of learning may look like this. A student answers an exam question, mistakes the meaning of the command word 'describe' and instead 'explains'. As a result, the student does not answer the question. Through written or verbal comments, the teacher points the student in the right direction and they are able to improve their answer. After acting on feedback, the student should write on their bookmark a suitable feedforward target. In this instance, an appropriate target for future exam practice might be 'Double-check the meaning of the command word in a question'. You could even get learners to write down key success criteria for future targets such as 'Highlight the command word' and 'Check the command word display before answering the question'.

The beauty of recording targets on a bookmark is that bookmarks can be moved from one exam question to the next, from one finished exercise book to a new exercise book, even from one subject to another and from the exercise book into the hall for mock exams. By keeping the outcomes of incisive feedback literally in front of a student's eyes, it acts as a constant reminder as to what they can be focusing on to become even better in your subject.

Regularly using bookmarks in lessons makes them an integral part of a routine for learning. For instance,'planner out', 'exercise book out' and 'bookmark out' can encourage students to take ownership of their own progress.

Bookmarks are also useful for parents. Instead of parents having to scavenge through their child's book to find ways in which they can offer support, they can find all their child's targets in one place! It makes for a very functional conversation at parents' evening.

> **Bonus idea** ★
>
> Use feedforward targets as a way of arranging seating plans or grouping students for activities. Match up students according to shared strengths and weaknesses.

An honest review

'I was worried I was being too lenient, and it turns out I was right.'

Taking this approach to marking removes any favouritism and helps ensure you are marking fairly and that students genuinely understand their learning.

Like most teachers you will have favourites, and while we aim to mark impartially, sometimes our views of students can cloud judgement. Even the most scrupulous teacher may be subconsciously over- or under-marking students' work. This can particularly be the case with the top grade 7–9 students – the type who has a halo and never puts a foot wrong, or the kind who puts so much effort into everything that you may be inclined to reread their work looking for extra marks so that they hit their target grade. You are doing them no favours.

For the next exam question a class completes, mark it blindly. Make sure you do not know who each exam question belongs to. There are several ways you can go about doing this:

- Get students to stack their books up at the end of the lesson, open on the page that contains the exam question you are going to mark.
- Give students lined paper and ask them to write their name on the back.
- Give each student a number to use instead of writing their name.

Employing this technique every so often ensures that your marking isn't biased and remains impartial. Students will actually feel rewarded knowing what they have achieved. It might even make weaker students try harder knowing that they are going to be judged impartially.

Question mats

'Having questions in front of me every day helped me to get used to how they're written.'

Question mats can come in many forms. They are essentially one piece of paper on which a series of typical exam questions are asked.

On the morning or night before an exam, students can end up stuck under a pile of paper, hectically trying to read through it all, retaining very little and panicking a lot. Giving them a question mat can be a good way to avoid this and make their exam morning as calm and stress-free as possible.

Question mats could be set up as a table, grid, tessellated shapes or flow diagrams of linked questions students can answer. Laminate and place them on student tables as a handy starter or plenary activity. You could even print them out as a way for students to shrink all of their required knowledge for an exam onto one single sheet of paper.

The most important thing is to use question mats well in advance of the exams, and the ways in which they can be used must be modelled to students before they can practise using them on their own. If you wait until a few weeks before the exam to give students such tools, then many will dismiss them.

Make sure you regularly put copies of these on the students' desks and use them in your lessons. Print them out double-sided: on one side the questions, on the reverse the answers. You can then let students chat through the answers or get them to write down a few answers at a time. If students become familiar with this resource, there is more likelihood of them using it as part of their revision.

Teaching tip

Use actual exam questions on your question mats – it sneaks in extra practice. If you set up these question mats in a grid, they can then easily be chopped up to make mini question cards.

Bonus idea

Why not get students to answer as many questions as quickly as they can?

Targeted starters

'It helped students focus on their individual weaknesses.'

A valuable practice is to start students off with a set of targeted questions as starters — this works particularly well after students have completed a past paper. Based on how students have performed, create a series of different questions linked to individual student weaknesses, e.g. things that students can't do — yet!

Taking it further

From January through to May of Year 11, plan what knowledge and skills you are going to revisit and how you are going to revisit them each week, either through a starter or through homework.

The value of frequent practice and using starters to regularly revisit key skills such as numeracy has been covered elsewhere in this book (see Idea 54). Get in the habit of setting differentiated starters as part of your regular teaching practice. Why not brand it in a way that students come to expect as part of their regular practice? For example, using their own revision checklist, you might implement a differentiated starter such as a 'Throwback Thursday', 'Memory Monday' or 'Think it back Tuesday', whereby on that particular day, students can choose or be directed to revisiting an area of the specification that they are weak in. A quick-fire quiz or revision activity to recap is ideal for this.

The underpinning purpose of any of these activities is to give students a regular opportunity to revisit their knowledge after a gap and also to prastise the things they can't do... yet. It is a proven way to help students retrieve previous learning so they have a better chance of remembering it!

If you have to do
it after school,
make it count

Part 9

Take your PIC

'This quick fix makes it manageable to help every student.'

Based on the long-standing idea of a revision checklist, a progress and intervention checklist (PIC) is a one-stop shop that provides a list of 'must revise' exam content, along with instant intervention activities.

A progress and intervention checklist (PIC) is a straightforward tool that can reduce the time it takes to plan and prepare a first-wave intervention. Designed to be used as a learning tool in the classroom, PICs allow teachers to track the progress students make in developing their exam knowledge and refining their skills, and enables them to rapidly respond to and intervene with those still grappling with key ideas or skills. Keeping true to the concept of the humble checklist, a PIC is a basic table made up of four columns:

Column 1: The first column should break down (in student-friendly language) the exam skills and knowledge to be mastered for the exam – one piece of content or one skill per row.

Column 2: Next is a column designed to allow for students to self-assess and track their own progress. This enables them to rate their understanding and confidence in a particular piece of knowledge or skill. Self-assessment works best if it quantifies how students might feel if something were to come up in their real exam. For instance, statements such as 'I would be happy if this was in the exam' or 'I would hate this to come up in the exam. I need to revisit this' are great for this column.

Column 3: Next to the columns for self-assessment, there should be space for detailing intervention – you can jot down activities that students can complete to improve in a particular skill or area of knowledge. The critical feature of this column is that it must signpost students to where and how they can go about revisiting the content independently. In addition, it should contain an activity that allows students to demonstrate their understanding once they have revisited the content. For instance, if a student was finding it tricky to explain the cause behind the 2004 Boxing Day tsunami, the intervention activity on the PIC could be signposting the student to a weblink of a video that explains the causes of the tsunami in a different way to the original explanation. After the student watches the video, they could then follow this up by sketching out a diagram to explain why tsunamis happen, using the information from the weblink. These intervention activities can handily double-up as revision exercises, homework or challenge tasks too! Intervention activities can be identified by the learner or teacher or even recommended by a peer. If a student still doesn't understand then this can be a trigger for further intervention.

Column 4: The final column of a PIC should allow for the class teacher to communicate how they feel the student is progressing. Some students might be over-generous in their self-assessment of what they think they know. Allowing the teacher to update the PIC can also help affirm what the student needs to do to ensure that they are exam-ready. This makes it simple for teachers, parents and students to keep track of progress made.

The best and most functional PICs are those that are planned by groups of teachers together. Suggest to your head of department that your next departmental meeting has the single-item agenda of working together to create a PIC. It will reduce planning and preparation in the long run and allow for intervention to go on in the classroom rather than wasting time running extra lunch or after-school sessions! A sample PIC is provided in the online resources for this book.

Taking it further

When marking books or providing live feedback, seek out your most vulnerable students first and check their PIC as a priority. Don't risk their books being at the bottom of a pile of 30, knowing that when you are marking and reviewing them you will have probably lost the will to live, let alone mark!

Bonus idea ★

Create a gigantic copy for the wall of a corridor or classroom.

Can-do corridors

'Some students will line up along a corridor no fewer than six times a day. Teamed with lesson transitions, corridors are hot property.'

School corridors: students wander them, line up along them, sit along them and occasionally are sent outside to stand in them! This idea will help you to turn them into valuable spaces.

Before reading this, take a walk along the corridors directly outside your classroom. Like most schools, the corridor will probably have gleaming examples of Key Stage 3 students' work furnishing the walls. Take the challenge to include examples of model Key Stage 4 work. Create your very own can-do corridor!

Aim to enlarge examples of great GCSE work and display it along the corridor. Make sure you annotate it with what makes it grade 9 worthy so that other students can see it. Team it with a photo of the student creating the work to attract attention to the display. If you have reprographics provision, see whether they can blow these up for you.

Here are some other ways to use displays:

- Put up ideas of how to answer certain types of questions.
- Blow up specialist terms and emblazon these along the corridor.
- Create an exam and revision display.
- Signpost students to useful information or people.
- Display front covers of the exam so students become familiar with its appearance.
- Put up details of when their exam is going to be and whether there are any revision sessions.

Toilet tricks

'Let the brainwashing begin!'

If the words 'go compare' were mentioned, there's a pretty good chance the TV ad image of a jolly opera singer with a moustache would pop into your head. There's an even better chance you might find yourself humming the annoying song. The next idea builds on the same principle – recurrence.

Everyone uses the toilet. That's the nature of the human body. When you've used a public toilet, you'll probably have noticed that on the inside of the toilet door there is almost always a snap frame containing an advert of some sort. It just so happens that the advert is smack-bang in front of your face while you are doing your business. With no escape, there is a pretty good chance that while stationary most people will give it a glance. Why not steal this idea and try it at your school?

Go through your exam content and glean from it any diagrams or key ideas and turn them into a poster for the loos! Even better, save yourself the job and get your students to each make a poster for their homework. Give learners very explicit success criteria to ensure posters are readable and exam-relevant.

While snap frames in every toilet around school could be costly, double-sided tape provides a cheaper alternative and works just as well. Don't forget, students should also be washing their hands after every toilet trip. Capitalise and put posters up near the hand dryers and mirrors too.

Every so often, update the posters and be safe in the knowledge that during the average four trips a day a student makes to the toilet, they will be putting the time to good use – even if it is while reapplying mascara!

Teaching tip

Don't forget you will need to take these posters down from toilets used during the exam season!

Taking it further

Why not make your students a starter quiz based on the posters up in the toilets to monitor whether they are having an impact?

Bank of past papers

'I just assumed everyone knew how to access past papers.'

Past paper practice is essential. If students know how to answer exam questions and have practised this, they will undoubtedly find the exam much easier and hopefully avoid the risk of making silly rubric errors.

Teaching tip

Offering to mark any practice questions students complete will take a huge chunk of your time but it will make a huge difference. Think about giving students a list of the types of questions they should be practising.

Taking it further

Do parents know where they can download past papers for students to complete? Tell them. Include this in the information you give parents at parents' evening or in any communications sent home.

Bonus idea ★

If your school printing budget is super tight and there is no wiggle room, consider selling packs of past papers or get a prefect to copy and paste questions from exam papers onto one document, from which students can write practice answers onto lined paper.

Ask yourself the following questions: Do students know where they can get past papers from? Can students download past papers directly from their school website? Is there an easy way for them to print these off if they don't have a printer at home? Make past papers as accessible as possible and make sure you have posters up reminding students of this and refer to it where possible in lessons.

Think about your typical disaffected or lazy student. Printing off past papers might in some cases just be too much effort, and the likelihood is that some students just aren't going to bother.

Consider whether there is any way for you to give out examples of past papers and mark schemes to students. Give every student at least one copy of an exam paper and related mark scheme. Like a library, make the offer to students that if they complete the exam paper, you will mark it and they can then take away a different past paper. This is a way of providing everyone with an example of a past paper but also ensuring that those students who do use them as part of their revision can then access more and benefit from having their teacher cast an eye over their exam practices.

Ten-minute takeover

'Intervention doesn't always have to be an hour after school.'

If it becomes clear that a student hasn't grasped something in your lesson and if your school day allows it, keep that student behind and revisit what they don't know. But be strict on yourself and limit it to just ten minutes, as nobody wants to stay at school longer than they have to.

Make ten-minute takeovers as engaging as possible, with the sole learning goal being that students have to demonstrate that they understand whatever it is they don't know by the end of the ten minutes.

If a student hasn't grasped something in your lesson, there is no point revisiting it in the same way. You have to mix it up. A favourite is to revisit a topic and then get the student to prove they know it by drawing or writing an explanation on the table with a whiteboard pen. The rebellious side of the student will enjoy writing on the table.

If you have a progress board up in your classroom, make a space on it for writing the names of the students who need to attend a ten-minute takeover, along with the thing that they need to revisit. When students attend, put a timer on the board so you are done within the ten-minute slot (as long as learners can prove they have got it).

Most schools have it written into their behaviour policy that you can keep students behind after lessons for a set amount of time, so use this to your advantage. If a student needs extra help, you are entitled to keep them for this amount of time.

> **Bonus idea** ★
>
> Send students away with an additional 'prove it' practice or 'fix it' to ensure that their learning is secure.

Booster sessions

'The ones I really wanted to speak to never came.'

Run smaller intervention booster sessions. Ideally the small group should have shared needs and work well together. Any booster sessions you choose to deliver should be targeted and should be by invitation only. The smaller the group, the greater the gains will be.

Many teachers feel pressurised into running additional after-school classes and typically it is the students who do not need to be there who usually turn up. When this happens, it can lead to achievement gaps widening, as top-end students attend, and disaffected students opt out.

When planning your booster sessions, you must be very clear on what the attendants can and can't do already. If you just run these sessions based on guesswork, they will not be targeted enough to make a difference. The earlier you run these sessions the better.

- Before organising a booster session, you must work out who your attendants are going to be. These might be picked out for you by SLT or your head of department. If you are free to put together your own group, determine who should be there from assessment outcomes in lessons.
- Keep the atmosphere relaxed. No one wants to stay after school if they don't need to.
- Fuel your session with healthy treats to make it more bearable.
- Organise your booster sessions so that students do not have to write a great deal.
- Include revision as part of the session, creating a revision tool that students can take away and use as part of their actual revision.
- Students must demonstrate their understanding to escape from the room!.

Teaching tip

Whatever you organise, remember you do not need to organise additional after-school sessions for the sake of it. You need to avoid becoming burnt out as this will impact on your teaching during the day.

Taking it further

If students are struggling with several key concepts, consider putting on a carousel activity for students to revisit a different key concept with a different teacher.

Bonus idea ★

Immerse students in a range of learning styles. For instance, if disaffected students are attending, use the power of music, video, talk and group work to jolt them into action.

Personal training

'Putting the emphasis on the student gave them control of their learning.'

Make your students plan their own after-school sessions!

For a lot of teachers, extra sessions can mean having to plan and teach an additional session on top of the five or six lessons they are already delivering on a daily basis. On the other hand, what do students have to do? Turn up. What a good deal.

Think about personal training sessions delivered at a gym. The focus of the sessions is always placed on the client. When you turn up to a personal training session, the personal trainer's first question is 'What do you want to achieve?' This approach should be taken with students, too. If you run a session, put the onus on the student. If the student wants your time and your expertise, they have to attend the revision session with something that they want to look at. They should not expect you to deliver something all singing, all dancing. This would have been provided for them the first time round in their actual lesson.

Replace your typical revision session with a doctor's surgery-style approach. If a student has a problem, they can either drop in or book an appointment but they must show up with a problem that requires solving. This might be a past paper question they are struggling with, queries over how to do something linked to a particular skill, or questions linked to revision. Advertise your one-to-one sessions so that students know they are happening. If a student needs intervention that can't be delivered in class, provide them with a regular slot too.

> **Bonus idea** ★
>
> Work with other members of your department. When you book in at the doctor's surgery, it can be pot luck which practitioner you get to see. Sometimes hearing ideas explained by a fresh face can really help students. Similarly, when you phone the doctor you are typically given an appointment with a triage nurse first, then if the problem is deemed serious enough you will be referred to the doctor. Why not tap up your Level 7–9 students for this triage role?

Tap into form time

'The extra 20 minutes of teaching time was invaluable.'

All too often the burden of intervention falls on teachers either after school or over lunchtime. The end result can be a set of very hungry and exhausted teachers. The focus should be on quality-first teaching as a first wave of intervention, followed by explicit opportunities built into the existing timetabled school day. A solution could lie in making better use of form time.

You (and most teachers) will more than likely hold a pastoral responsibility of being a form tutor. Time is therefore taken up in the mornings with tutor group activities such as literacy and numeracy work, team-building activities and assembly.

Looking at this arrangement with a fresh pair of eyes, do you need to attend assembly? Could a better use of your time be to sit down with a student and deliver a one-to-one booster session on something they can get to grips with in this timeframe? Could it be an option to suggest that a heavyweight member of SLT sit in assembly instead, thus freeing up teacher time for intervention first thing in the morning? If this was arranged for every year-group assembly, imagine the impact of every teacher in school having an extra 20 minutes of one-to-one time with a student who needs a little boost.

For a short period, could Key Stage 3 forms be given two assemblies a week to free up even more teacher time for intervention?

Bonus idea ★

If your school operates a vertical pastoral system whereby form groups are made up of a mixture of students from different key stages, could Year 11s be transferred between forms to the teacher who could help them the most? Or could staff without form responsibilities be set up as super tutors?

Intervention booklets

'This is a useful way to ensure students grasp how to answer exam questions.'

Use past papers to make up a booklet of exam questions. Ideally these should map your specification and cover the necessary range of knowledge and skills required for the final exam. Include a variety of different types of exam question. This might comprise an assortment of questions that are of differing lengths or a range of questions covering the multitude of command words that a student might be exposed to.

The end game of most GCSE courses is for a student to be successful in an exam. This requires students to be able to do several things. First, they need to be able to respond correctly to exam language. Second, they must be able to apply or link the correct knowledge or skills to each individual question. Some students could require support for either of these things, and how you use the exam question intervention booklets will be determined by your exam cohort.

One way that intervention booklets can be used is on a diagnostic basis. For instance, if after a lesson completing a practice question a student still appears to be struggling, then they could be directed to completing an additional practice question outside of the lesson. If after attempting this the student is still struggling, then this is an indicator that the student might require one-to-one tutoring on this particular part of the specification.

Bonus idea ★

These can also double up as handy practice questions for students to revisit as part of their revision.

Routines for revising at home

'Supported with the right guidance and knowledge, parents can help support revision at home.'

Students spend six hours a day in school. To secure exam success, it is imperative to equip students and parents alike with good routines to support quality revision at home.

As a teacher, it is important to ensure that both parents and students have the knowledge of what makes for effective revision at home. For example, a parent might see their child spending hours slaving away producing beautiful revision cards and be misled in thinking they are revising. Similarly, a parent might see their child spending hours in their bedroom 'revising', with the reality being that time is lost to gaming and social media. We know that many students do not work well with delayed gratification – with many opting to use their spare time on what they value there and then rather than what will benefit them later. But parents can help. As a minimum, put in practice the following ten things:

1 Remind parents of the need for children to have a good work space for revision, ideally a quiet and well-lit place to study away from distractions such as social media or the TV. It could be a good idea to encourage parents and their child to have a discussion about how their bedroom could be turned into more of a revision room for the short term.
2 Encourage parents to provide a supply of stationery for their child, e.g. revision cards, sticky notes, folders to organise revision, paper.
3 Recommend the right revision guides and provide a copy of a revision checklist.

4 Share with parents the importance of children having goals and checking in with their child to see how their revision is progressing – helping their child to manage their time, effort and emotions and, if needed, checking through the quality of revision materials or perhaps providing support in how these materials could be organised.

5 Tell parents about the theory of spaced revision rather than last-minute cramming and encourage parents to support their child in creating a revision timetable and then monitoring it to ensure that students are having the right balance between work and rest.

6 Share with parents the importance of using past papers and make sure both the parent and child know the location of these, e.g. where these are saved on the school website.

7 Remind parents of the timing of any final parents' evenings, intervention or revision sessions and final exam dates.

8 Suggest it might be necessary to consider turning off the Wi-Fi at home and/or taking away their child's mobile phone while they are revising. Suggest an evening routine for this so everyone is clear on what should be happening – including revision breaks.

9 Encourage communication with the school. For instance, if their child is displaying signs of anxiety, make sure the parents let school know so that everyone can support the child in question.

10 Finally, share with parents the importance of taking an interest in their child's revision, especially the role that they can play in supporting young people with low-stakes quizzing of exam content.

Bonus idea ★

If you discover a pupil premium student doesn't have access to a desk, chair or revision materials, e.g. books or stationery, ask a member of SLT whether there is any funding available to provide these. You could suggest having a school 'revision room' that Year 11 can access before and after school for independent revision.

Exam questions for homework

'There just isn't enough time in class to practise as often as they need to.'

Exam practice is invaluable and building it up in a way that emulates the real exam has great merits for getting students exam-ready and checking their understanding.

On setting an exam question for homework, make sure you are prescriptive. First, clarify how much writing space students should be using. Provide students with an actual photocopy of the exam question, with the same style, size and amount of writing lines as they would have in the real exam, or prescribe how many lines in their exercise book their answers should use. It is important that students get used to how much they have to write. Weaker students may need pushing to extend points and write more, while top-end students may struggle to write succinctly in the amount of space available.

In addition to actual physical paper space, other exam variables that need considering when getting students to practise answering questions include the type of exam question and whether they use specific command or restricting words; the number of marks awarded for different types of questions; additional SPGST marks; the optional use of additional diagrams, photos or sources; and how much time is available to complete the exam question. Each variable can make for a great focus when completing practice questions. One way to start to work towards emulating exam conditions is to give students ownership of choosing what prompts they use when completing an exam question.

Flip the learning

'This little change made a big difference to how quickly we could get into the new learning.'

When setting homework, make sure it is either a flipped learning activity or a practice exam question. Aim to give one piece of homework a week and be clear about the consequences of not completing it.

The Sutton Trust-EEF Teaching and Learning Toolkit (see Idea 10) shows that homework makes a difference. You should therefore build it into your planning and focus on setting homework that provides students with the explicit opportunity to practise exam skills. Most students hate homework. They dislike having to sit down and spend time working outside of school and who can blame them? Whenever you set homework you no doubt hear the typical cries of: 'Not more homework' or 'I've been set so much already'. This is where having high expectations helps.

You must prioritise completing the learning for the exam course in lessons. Sometimes teaching time disappears and before you know it you can end up setting students new learning to complete at home just so they have touched upon all of the knowledge they need. This should be avoided at all costs. Instead, focus setting homework pieces on introducing students to new learning via a flipped activity. For instance, get them to do some pre-lesson reading and research or complete practice questions. Homework makes a difference. Flipped learning activities mean that students will arrive to your lesson with some prior learning (it almost allows you to fast-forward through the basics via well-placed connect activities).

Teaching tip

At the start of the GCSE course or at the beginning of every new term, share the outcomes of the Sutton Trust-EEF Teaching and Learning Toolkit with students. Show them in real terms what doing homework means. It has an impact.

Getting students revision-ready

Part 10

Revision journey

'Finding out what works.'

Every person is unique, and how each individual learns can also be very different. Revision journeys are a great way of tracking whether a particular type of revision has been successful for a student or whether they would be better using an alternative method for revisiting their learning.

Schools have become quite savvy in teaching students about the different ways to revise, such as mind-mapping, revision cards, posters, flash cards and past paper questions. What we are not so good at is helping students to reflect on what revision has worked and what hasn't. After students have sat a test, what do you do? Most teachers will unpick where students have gone wrong with a question, and the likelihood is very little focus is placed on problems with their revision.

Revision journeys are a way to ensure that students analyse their approach to an exam, not just their result. When they're reflecting and evaluating after an exam – particularly when they have been disappointed with the outcome – students are quick to say 'I needed to revise more' and all too often that response is accepted. Similarly, when are high-performing students forced to reflect on how successful their revision has been? After many exams, students are set two types of target: one for knowledge or skills to be practised, and another that focuses on exam technique. Very rarely are students set targets linked to improving the revision that will underpin their performance. Revision journeys consider the actions students took in the run-up to their exam and the outcomes of their exam. It is an easy way to capture whether or not the type of revision a student has invested time in has paid off.

Revision-ready

'Exercise books are so much better than mass-produced revision guides.'

The best position for students to be in – well in advance of the exam season – is revision-ready. They must have everything in place and a revision checklist can help them achieve this.

While teachers do have a role to play in coordinating this, the focus should be on students investing their time in making sure they are prepared for their revision. A way to achieve this is by having a revision checklist stuck on the front of every one of your students' books or folders. The checklist should be a set of instructions listing things they should be getting ready during their time on the course. See the online resources for a sample checklist.

Sticking the checklist in the front of every student's exercise book makes sure that every student is consciously focused on the end game. Ideally, put one of these on the *front* of every exercise book your students use. It is the perfect reminder to them that they will be sitting an exam and they have to be prepared for it! Being prepared will hopefully mean that students will actually spend more time revising than colouring in things like revision timetables!

Bonus idea ★

Give students the time to prepare before completing the revision checklist. This doesn't need to be during lesson time. Set it for homework. You could complete the same checklist after the student and see whether you agree with each other's assessment of how revision-ready they are.

Model active revision

'I thought having my books open was enough but it wasn't. I needed to actively revise.'

One of the mistakes we make as teachers is to assume students know how to revise.

Experience tells us that reading and highlighting notes has minimal impact. What actually makes learning stick is active revision. There are stacks of tools that students can use to revise. Here is a list of handy revision strategies that students should be using in the run-up to their exams:

- revision cards
- flash cards
- mind maps
- shrinking learning down into lists
- A–Z of things linked to a topic
- picture reminders
- past paper questions
- dominoes – to match up keywords and meanings
- hexagons – to show relationships between knowledge by tessellating the shape
- graphic organisers
- pairs and snap
- say it and remember it
- write words or facts in the air
- origami revision tools such as decision makers or revision foldables.

The best thing to do as a teacher is to model these activities wherever you can in lessons, demonstrating to students how these different tools can be used to answer past papers. Then remind students that these are tools and ideas that they could be using as part of their own independent revision at home.

One of the most effective ways to make learning stick is to get students to teach each other. Consider putting revision into a sequence for students. They should start by manipulating their notes using one or more of the revision tools above, shrinking down the key ideas or concepts. Ideally, students must then do something active with these tools to truly make the learning stick. My favourite is to encourage students to look at their learning for a few minutes and then get them to cover it up and see how much of it they can remember, either by saying it out loud or by writing down the knowledge and ideas they have been able to retain.

However students choose to revise, don't forget to ensure that they reflect on the success of their revision after practice tests to ascertain whether their choice of revision worked for them.

> **Bonus idea** ★
>
> Students could play the examiner and create their own test paper using a list of command words and the exam specification. Students should write model answers to go with the questions or provide guidance for any candidates answering the questions.

Total recall

'Makes it easy to remember knowledge.'

For many years, Marie Nevard (@Marie_Nevard) has built regular data memory training into her lessons as a vital piece of the exam success puzzle, enabling all students to maximise their potential. Regular data memory training is a vital piece of the exam success puzzle, enabling all students to maximise their potential.

The ability to memorise data and detail is a key skill to master for exam students of all ages. Some common marking criteria for top-grade answers include 'clear evidence of detailed examples', 'facts or figures are used to support explanations' and 'judgements are supported by evidence throughout'. For many students it seems an impossible task to remember all the finer details; however, with some regular and basic training they are always amazed at how much they can memorise and how quickly.

There are a number of tools and techniques that can be used to aid memory recall.

Memory drills

Going back to basics and drilling students on a regular basis throughout the school year proves to be highly successful. It leads to more detailed and specific exam answers, as well as an improvement in students' confidence in their own ability to memorise key facts and figures. Create a worksheet outlining the main data and specific details you would like to be memorised by the whole class.

Drill them in order of the sheet at first and then in a mixed-up fashion to increase the challenge and keep all students engaged. Students can continue to memorise it at home, ready for weekly or fortnightly quick mini-tests throughout the weeks and months before their exam. These can be quick verbal drills, written tests or worksheets with gaps to fill in. The repeated nature of this task means the information is easily embedded in students' minds come exam time, which helps minimise stress levels and also enables them to focus on other important matters such as learning the main syllabus content, developing their writing skills and answering questions under a time limit.

Memory worksheets

Students can create their own memory worksheet for a topic in groups or as a class. The data and facts from teacher- or student-created memory worksheets can be used by students to make and/or complete further revision tasks, including:

- **Triominoes** – Students match a set of triangle dominoes using linking facts, figures, key terms and definitions. This can create a hexagon shape or other pattern. Tarsia software can be used to create these patterns. Tutor2U also have many fantastic activity templates, including one for tridominoes.
- **Infographics** – Students can create informative and visual infographics for revision using key facts, figures and images. Useful websites include www.infogr.am, www.easel.ly and www.piktochart.com.
- **Animated videos and presentations** – Using websites such as www.powtoon.com and www.prezi.com and apps such as Apple's 'Stop Motion Studio', students can use important information and data to create engaging animations and presentations to teach their class.

Revision cards

'They were beautiful, but they were useless.'

Revision cards are not a new phenomenon but how students use them needs to be built into your everyday teaching if they are to be part of a successful revision plan. All too often students are encouraged to make these tools and then only use them in the confines of their bedroom the night before their exam. In order for revision cards to be optimised, students need teaching and showing what a good revision card looks like and then how to use them as part of an active revision strategy.

Making revision cards is a no brainer. They are an effective way of shrinking down masses of handwritten notes into a form that is much more functional. You first need to decide whether you are going to make revision cards for your class or get students to create their own. Either way is fine; the important bit is how they are used. From the very start of the GCSE course, students should be crafting things like revision cards. All too often students will finish a GCSE course and then spend hours of their time making revision cards. Very often the students mistake this activity for revising, when making revision cards is really part of the preparation for revision, not revision itself. How the cards are used and how frequently is what will make the difference.

Model to students what a functional revision card looks like. Encourage students to put the knowledge they need to learn on one side and then prompt questions on the reverse. Teach them how to use the exam specification to locate exactly what they need to be revising – or provide them with a clear list.

Make sure students know how to use revision cards. If possible, give them a set of instructions like the following:

Step 1 – Choose an exam question to answer.

Step 2 – Write down everything you know about the exam question already.

Step 3 – Read through the relevant revision cards – highlight on the revision card anything they you had forgotten.

Step 4 – After reading through the revision cards, use them to answer the exam question. To make this more challenging, try to answer the exam question without relooking at the revision cards.

Other uses of revision cards:

- On the reverse of every revision card write out some quick-fire questions. Get a peer or parent to test you using the questions. Or if you are trying to remember dates, put the event on one side and the date on the reverse.
- Look – Cover – Write; Look – Cover – Witter.
- Use the revision cards to write your own exam question.
- Use the revision cards to create your own games, e.g. once you have memorised a card, turn it into a card house.
- Stick them up around the house in key places where you will read them.
- Stick one in your phone case to read when you are out and about.
- Take photos of your revision cards on your phone so you can revise on the go.
- Shrink your revision cards down into another format such a mind map.
- Create one last-minute revision card of the things you are finding the trickiest to remember.

Bonus idea ★

At the start of a topic, give your students a set of blank mini revision cards that they can create as they learn.

Quick quiz

'This is a perfect activity for revisiting knowledge.'

Students are sent into exams having to regurgitate knowledge that is from up to two years ago. Can you even remember what you were doing two years ago? It is essential to create opportunities for students to revisit their prior learning in order to avoid having to learn everything all over again. Quick quizzes are one tool that can make this happen.

Teaching tip

Always make sure the quizzes are marked – self-, peer- or teacher-assessed – so that they provide a useful tool for revision.

Taking it further

After a student has completed a quiz, the opportunity for them to apply the knowledge from the quiz to a longer extended answer is also a useful activity. Don't just limit quick quizzes to the classroom. Set them as homework too. Or give students sections of the specification and get them to make their own.

Bonus idea ★

Try setting up your quick quizzes online. There are lots of great free websites you can use to create quizzes, e.g. www.onlinequizcreator.com and http://quizstar.4teachers.org/.

Your approach to this activity can vary and mixing it up a bit will keep students on their toes. Give your class a quick quiz regularly, once a week ideally. Give students ten questions to answer. The quiz should take no more than ten minutes, with each question being the equivalent of a one- to two-mark exam question.

Create a ten-by-two grid and give students the questions typed out to answer. Using this method ensures the quiz can be reused as part of future revision. You could read out the questions instead. Don't forget it's labelled a quiz: students can therefore complete it individually or in teams. If you want to get students to answer longer, more extended questions, still stick to the idea of a 'quick' quiz but give them fewer questions to answer.

It can prove handy to keep a copy of the specification and highlight things that you revisit using a quick quiz. You should aim to revisit learning at least three times if you can.

You may choose to give students the homework task of revising for the quiz or just spring it on them as a surprise. There is value in both approaches so mix it up. Try setting a series of quizzes for the different GCSE grades and give students the choice over which quiz they take.

Bin the bag

'Reduce, reuse and revise!'

The best way of guaranteeing that students are exam-ready is making revision active and revisiting topics at every opportunity. Setting up a revision folder is a no-nonsense way of achieving this.

The last exam season saw the birth of a new craze: the rise of the revision goodie bag. The concept is essentially a bag filled to the brim with resources to help and motivate students to revise in the run-up to their final exam. After our results came out last year, we spent time reflecting and unpicking what actually made the difference. The impact of my well-thought-out and caring bags? Zilch! There is a role for revision resources and more about these can be found in the rest of Part 10. But the thing that makes a much bigger difference to exam outcomes is upskilling students in how to effectively use exam revision aids.

So, going forward, bin the bag! Instead, take all the lovely resources and revision materials you are planning to put together and don't wait – issue them to students as soon as you can and ask students to build their revision folders over time. The earlier you start this, the better. Don't wait to gift them as a final goodbye. It is also sensible not to overload learners with everything all at once. If students do not value the materials you give them, they will not use them. If the typical party bag is anything to go by, students will probably only eat the sweets!

Teaching tip

If you have the space, keep revision folders in your classroom and dip into them regularly as part of your lesson plans.

Taking it further

Drip-feed your students revision tools. Build in the opportunity within lessons to use the different tools, be it revision cards, flash cards or revision booklets, etc. Better still, get students to make their own so they truly value the hard work that has gone into them.

Build an assessment

'This is a sneaky way to do a full exam paper over a series of lessons.'

One of the things many students hate is having to do exam practice. Aside from extrinsic bribes, if you want students to complete exam questions frequently you have to adapt your approach. This is necessary to avoid lessons becoming static. One approach that can be used in a variety of ways is to build an assessment over a series of lessons.

This can be used in the same way a popular retail store makes cuddly creatures. A series of stations is set up, but instead of building up a bear, you replace it with an exam question. Dependent on your type of exam, you could set up your classroom as a series of stations that students must move around to build an answer. This might include using materials at different stations to answer different questions or creating different paragraphs at each station to build up an extended answer. Getting students up and about can help engage disaffected students, jolting them into action at the excitement of being able to escape the confines of their usual desk. You could even get students to move between the stations accompanied by music to liven it up.

An alternative approach is to do this over a series of lessons. This is great for subjects where students are asked questions of varying length in their exam. For instance, in geography exams, students have to answer a range of two-mark to nine-mark questions for a total of 25 marks. Why not give students exam questions in the same way you might use exit tickets? Over a course of lessons, give students a different exam question to answer in order to escape the room. The power of escape is a great tool, especially if your lesson is before break-time or at the end of the day.

Last one standing

'This activity can start a lesson on a high.'

A twist on the quick quiz (Idea 88), the last one standing is a quiz whereby each question increases in difficulty.

Make this game high-stakes and link it to target grades or reward with chocolate. Start with easy questions that would typically be worth one or two marks in the exam paper and then build it up to more challenging questions. The student who is able to answer the most questions within a given time frame is awarded the accolade of last one standing.

Obviously the more fun you make this, the more likely students are to engage. Introduce the quiz using something that students want and are prepared to play for. For maximum impact, set your classroom up in the style of a quiz show. Put up a cringe worthy slide on your projector and play a cheesy theme tune as students enter your room. As with a variety of game shows, you could set contestants to work in isolation or in small groups to win the ultimate prize and to be the last one standing.

Give your all to playing the role of the game show host. Students love it (or are at least engaged) when their teacher is trying to act cool. Then rattle through as many questions as you can. You might want to get students to answer the questions on mini-whiteboards (at least for the easier rounds). Get them to answer each question holding their answers up in an instant 'reveal' fashion, for which they can self-assess. Alternatively, get a class member to act as the scorer.

> **Bonus idea** ★
>
> Share all of the questions with students and give them a set amount of time. Allow students to answer the questions in any order so that they can set their own level of challenge.

Tackle the beast

'The exam paper was so unwieldy, it kept falling off the table.'

In an exam, students are under pressure and mistakes are a hazard of the game. 'Tackle the beast' is a strategy to deliberately cause students to make these mistakes in your lessons first, so that they don't repeat the same mistakes in their real exam.

While mock exams can go some way to emulating exam conditions, one of the things teachers should do at the very start of the course is to give students a full copy of an exam paper, including any resource booklets that may be part of the exam. The more contact students have with the full exam, the more confident they will feel in tackling the beast. Don't skimp by photocopying just the sections of the exam students have to answer. Give them an identical copy of a full real exam.

Draw attention to even the most basic things about the exam paper, e.g. important instructions that only appear on the front cover and how to find the relevant questions in those papers that give students a choice of topics.

It is useful to give students the opportunity to get to grips with the physical nature of the paper. Often exam papers consist of huge amounts of pages along with additional resource booklets. Students need experience in manoeuvring around all of this! Even familiarity with the tiniest details, such as knowing their candidate number and centre number, will help – completing this first administrative task correctly will reduce any potential flapping and help keep students calm in the exam.

Regularly mock

'The more exam practice a student does, the more likely they are to succeed.'

Like tricky Zumba moves, the more students practise the complex business of exams, the more confident they will be when it comes to the final event.

One of the trickiest things for students to get right is exam timing, but the good news is this can be practised anywhere. At the start of the qualification, learners will obviously need longer to complete exam practices. But as you approach the exam, students need to be placed under the same time pressures as they are actually going to face. To help students with this, get a replica of the clock that is up in the exam hall and then, for whatever exam question students are doing, give them the same amount of time they would have in the real exam. Deal with timing in the same way the real invigilators will do. For instance, write the time students have to complete their exam onto the board and imitate the half-hourly reminders invigilators give students. For the longer questions, build in the opportunities for students to practise self-monitoring their own timing; encourage them to write down longer exam questions or work out how long different sections of the paper took them to complete so they can look back at this on their next practice paper and try to make gains.

Think about other exam conditions you could emulate in your classroom. For instance, choosing not to help students or to answer any questions, making them write in the same colour pen prescribed by the exam, sitting students on individual desks or making students enter the room and sit down in absolute silence to start an exam.

Teaching tip

Build in time so that students can carry out their own review of their mock exam. Download my '5 minute Exam Review' planning tool from www.teachertoolkit.co.uk/wp-content/uploads/2018/01/5-min-exam-review.pptx.

Taking it further

Try setting students targets for exam timing. For instance, spend 30 seconds skimming your answer for use of specialist terms, or spend one minute pulling your answer together with a conclusion.

Bonus idea ★

Explore how easy it would be to take your class into the same space in which they will sit their final exam. Could the same room be booked for your lesson time? Get students so used to completing work at an exam desk that it feels like the norm.

Getting students exam-ready

Part 11

Ways of building teacher capacity

'We're a team – we're in it together.'

During the spring term in the run-up to final exams, teacher workload explodes! Everyone is busy and everyone is undoubtedly working extremely hard but considering staff as a collective when it comes to intervening with students is a sure-fire way to build in capacity and could make a real difference.

The strategy employed here will really depend on the school need and people's talents. But a good way to secure progress is to pull together as a whole school.

One way of building in capacity is to look at the role of teaching assistants (TAs) in supporting intervention. While the burden of delivering revision sessions shouldn't fall on TAs for individual subjects, they can definitely support students in being more organised and revision-ready. This could be through supporting students with getting revision materials together or orchestrating opportunities for completing supervised exam question practice. This shouldn't be just for weaker-ability students but for any student who struggles with their organisation.

Why not attach a TA to every department during the spring term? During this time, the TA will be able to support teachers wherever possible and wherever needed. For instance, teachers could direct TAs to differentiating resources ready for their classes, freeing up teacher time to focus on Year 11. Or who says a TA can't tick and flick through a set of books marking for literacy, regardless of the subject?

SWOT it

'I could see clearly where to focus my efforts in the final push.'

A SWOT analysis tool is used to collate and reflect on strengths, weaknesses, opportunities and threats. Ask students to carry out their own SWOT analysis at key checkpoints in their learning.

Here's an example of what students might include in their SWOT analysis:

Strengths: Specific topics or skills; exam technique or types of exam question; revision preparedness; organisation; classwork and homework; attributes as a learner, e.g. behaviour, effort and engagement in learning.
Weaknesses: Specific topics or skills; exam technique or types of exam question; revision preparedness; organisation; classwork and homework; attributes as a learner, e.g. behaviour, effort and engagement in learning. What could you improve? What types of revision should you avoid? What things in the exam lose you marks?
Opportunities: How could you get extra marks in the exam? What strategies could you use? What actions could you take now to improve your exam performance?
Threats: What threatens your possible exam grade? What are the barriers to your learning? To your success?

When students are completing their SWOT, they should be precise in their statements, basing their ideas on evidence from practice exam questions or teacher feedback. After students have completed their own SWOT, get them to devise ways of eliminating any of the threats they have picked out. Give students strategies to use to overcome threats, or steps that they can take to limit the damage to their exam achievement.

Teaching tip

SWOTs can be very powerful for identifying marginal gains. They are particularly useful as they can help learners manage and eliminate risks or threats to exam grades: things that would otherwise catch them unawares.

Bonus idea ★

Complete your very own SWOT for your class.

Bare necessities

'It helped to calm her down and reassure her that she did have some knowledge.'

Stripping down exam content onto one A3 table mat makes last-minute revision possible.

Prepare in advance for the occasion when your student arrives the morning before their exam confessing and stressing about the fact that they haven't done the amount of revision they should have. There are also circumstances where a student's nerves have just got the better of them and they have gone into panic mode. In some instances, students may even have struggled with back-to-back exams and literally been flying by the seat of their pants.

The best strategy for dealing with last-minute wobbles is to calm the student down and remind them, using evidence from their prior learning in lessons, just what they are capable of. The next best thing you can do is to strip the content of the exam right down. Prepare in advance of exam day an A3 table mat with the bare minimum that might just help students to scrape a pass. Have these materials set up in a classroom somewhere quiet away from other students and be on hand to do some last-minute emergency coaching. Don't forget to get the site team to place a bin right in front of the door to the exam hall. Students can be looking at these sheets right up until the time they step foot into the room of doom!

Although superficial learning is not ideal, it is best to plan for the inevitable. You also don't want to scare students off from trying because in their heads they think they've failed before they've even sat the exam.

Before the exam

'It's a truly nerve-wracking time, but there is light at the end of the tunnel.'

There is little value in forcing knowledge down students in the hour before the exam. The most important thing is that they are entering the exam room with a winning mindset.

Before the exam there will be students who feel prepared and are ready to get on with it, there will be a group of students who are flapping and panicking, and then there will be the students who don't care.

In the time before the exam you should make sure you are available to calm any potential last-minute nerves. Ideally set up a series of rooms for students to go to. For instance, have a quiet classroom for individual revision and a different classroom for students who have last-minute questions about the exam. Don't worry about revising content as, at this point, it is too late.

Get as many teachers on hand as possible and focus on as many positive things as you can to provide a last-minute boost to students' self-confidence.

Make sure students have everything they require for the exam. Do they have what they need in their pencil case? If not, give it to them. Encourage good eating habits to make sure they are fully fuelled. Make sure students have a bottle of water. Students who have a bottle of water in the exam perform five per cent better. Teach your students good strategies for avoiding panic – for instance, if students start their exam and are confused by a question, encourage them to sit back, take a sip of water and then revisit it.

Teaching tip

One of the most useful things you can do is to scatter around past papers so that students can familiarise themselves with the layout of the papers and avoid rubric errors.

Taking it further

Put together suggestions for what parents can do pre-exam – e.g. the morning before – and post-exam to support their child. Pre- and post-exam care is important!

Bonus idea ★

If you are running a pre-exam session on the day of the exam, make it nice and light-hearted. Why not run a blueberry breakfast and tap into the useful antioxidants in the fruit? Have a slide show running of pictures from their lessons to act as triggers for their past learning.

Being a self-improving teacher

Part 12

The Buzz Breakfast

'It saves me time and keeps me "buzzing" with new ideas I can't wait to try in my classroom.'

Mike Mellors is the brains behind @FernwoodBUZZ, the Twitter feed that shares that idea of the 'Buzz Breakfast' – a very simple concept that can be implemented in any school (or organisation) to improve teaching across the school. The idea was originally shared at a teaching and learning meeting with Ellis Guilford School in Nottingham, where they wanted to provide more opportunities for staff to collaborate as a team.

Taking it further

The Buzz Breakfast can be tailored to the needs of the organisation. 'Closing the gap' has become a national focus and could really benefit the students you need to focus on. Staff could bring strategies and resources they have used that have had a real, positive impact on individual students. These could then be adapted to different subjects, helping to improve consistency across the board. The valuable 25-minute sessions could provide just the right opportunity for a group of teachers to discuss what they could do to help improve a student's understanding of another subject.

Within your school there is no doubt fantastic teaching happening daily, but do you always get to see it? As the demands on teachers increase, do you have the time to visit different classrooms and learn from each other? Do you want more ownership over your own CPD? Are you a member of SLT who wants to encourage and engage staff with their own CPD? This is where the Buzz Breakfast comes in.

How the Buzz Breakfast works: The Buzz Breakfast is a voluntary CPD session but provides the opportunity to collaborate across different subject areas. It can be organised as frequently as required – ideally on two different days every half-term. Run the session in the morning – for instance 5am (this can be changed depending on your school day).

Fuelled by coffee and croissants, the Buzz Breakfast takes a relaxed approach to improve teaching and learning for staff and students. During the sessions, staff are invited to talk, share and try new ideas.

Within the 25 minutes, invite staff to bring any ideas they have tried, discuss any ideas they have seen or just ask advice on any techniques or strategies they are looking to implement. This open platform provides staff with a powerful opportunity to collaborate with others across school. The government have always encouraged cross-curricular collaboration, and making links with other subjects has become more important than ever as we strive for consistency. The Buzz Breakfast allows staff to share resources and build on ideas that others have trialled.

Maths may have an assessment strategy that would work brilliantly in MFL, or geography may have an excellent starter activity that could be adapted and work perfectly for design and technology, but how would you know this unless you attended the Buzz Breakfast?

Numbers can fluctuate from session to session; however, greatness is contagious and teaching staff are no different. As staff begin to mention to others how the Buzz Breakfasts have helped them, more and more staff attend. Staff look forward to the sessions and can't wait to share what they have been up to.

Some faculties now have a Buzz Breakfast board where they stick up the ideas most appropriate to their faculty, while some staff write a Buzz Breakfast blog to feed ideas back to anyone who was unable to attend – a great way to support and help our teachers.

The Buzz Breakfast is a nice example of how voluntary CPD can make a difference to your staff and students.

Advice for running a Buzz Breakfast:

- Create a professional but relaxed brand image.
- Advertise in the staffroom.
- Tweet pictures of the sessions and the ideas that are shared to collaborate with other organisations.
- Have Buzz Breakfast boards in the staffroom and individual departments.

Bonus idea ★

Social media has gone from strength to strength in education. There are a growing number of 'Tweachers' sharing ideas daily. Consider setting up your own Twitter account just for researching great teaching and learning ideas. For instance, @FernwoodBUZZ Twitter account provides an invaluable way to team up with schools around the world. It is a great way of getting positive feedback on techniques, displays and assessment methods too.

What if it's still not working?

'All students are different and when it comes down to intervention one size does not fit all.'

Sometimes, no matter how hard you try as a teacher, some students can still fail to engage. The most important idea to follow here is not to waste your time trying to flog a dead horse, so to speak, either on an idea that just isn't making a difference or on a student who simply won't respond – occasionally, no matter how hard you try with a particular student, you continue to lose the ongoing battle. Sometimes it is worth admitting there may be that one student you cannot help, despite how much you care or how much you wish you could support them. The reality is you cannot sit a student's exam for them.

If you do find yourself in this situation then the test and learn approach can be a useful rule to follow to ensure that you leave no stone left unturned. Test and learn is a set of practices followed by retailers, whereby they test ideas with a small number of customers to foresee impact. The process is often designed to answer three questions about any idea before a full roll-out:

1 **What are you aiming to do?**
2 **What actions do you need to take?**
3 **What could be the impact?**

It is important to track your intervention, as if something isn't making the difference, it may be time to try something new. A good approach to take is to consider: What is not working? What should you stop doing? What is working – what should you continue doing? What should you start doing?

If nothing seems to be working, the most vital action to take is to speak up and share your concerns and frustrations. Talking to other people about your worries will make you feel better. This conversation might be with a pastoral head of year, your line manager or a teacher who teaches the same student or class. Do not get caught up in what you can't do; instead focus on what differences you can make. It is tricky but maintaining the approach of a glass half full is the most useful stance a teacher can take. Keep focused on what the bigger picture for your students actually is – helping them to build a better future for themselves – and then reflect on actions you can take each lesson to help them to work towards this. A student may not leave their time with you having obtained the grade you'd hoped for them, but even having you in their school life as a positive and caring role model will have an impact and will help students take a step towards having a better future. Keep focused on where your students are going and instil in them a self-belief, based on the expectations you have of them.

Bonus idea ★
Don't forget to look to social media for tweachers or teacher bloggers who regularly post new and fresh ideas online.

After the exam

'What will make the difference to next year's students?'

The time after an exam can provide an opportunity to reflect upon lessons learnt and ideas for action planning for future classes. Jot down ideas for anything you need to do differently for your next year's exam classes.

In most instances, the final exam can be just as stressful for the teacher. Find solace in asking yourself this question: 'What else could I have done to make a difference?' The answer will probably be very little.

Invite students up to your room after the exam for a bit of a debrief and to get their initial thoughts on how they feel they did. Don't allow them to panic; simply listen to any concerns they have and reiterate what great students they are, as they may have another exam later in the day. Then, as soon as possible, get your hands on an actual exam paper so you can contextualise any student concerns. If you are as impatient as I am, type your exam title into Twitter as soon as the exam is over – it is a great place to glean student and teacher responses from around the country. Jot down any common mistakes students say they have made; these can be really useful for informing your future planning.

After students have finished their exams, it can be worthwhile carrying out some student voice on what students thought went well and what they would change. This can be related to lessons, revision, exam preparation or exam technique. Always ask for their ideas for what might make a difference to them if they were starting their GCSEs again. It is a good idea to ask students to donate any revision materials or revision books if they are not carrying on with you on to A level.

Bonus idea ★

See whether your school has any money to employ Year 11s as peer mentors to your Year 10s throughout July. This can be a great opportunity to get your Year 10s up to speed for the start of Year 11.